Using Science to Develop Thinking Skills at Key Stage 3

Materials for Gifted Children

David Fulton Publishers

David Fulton Publishers Ltd
The Chiswick Centre, 414 Chiswick High Road, London W4 5TF

www.fultonpublishers.co.uk

First published in Great Britain in 2003 by David Fulton Publishers.
10 9 8 7 6 5 4 3 2 1

David Fulton Publishers is a division of Granada Learning Limited, part of Granada plc.

British Library Cataloguing in Publication Data
A catalogue record for this book is available from the British Library.

ISBN 1-84312-037-2

Typeset by FiSH Books, London
Printed and bound by Thanet Press

Contents

NACE National Office
PO Box 242
Arnolds Way
Oxford OX2 9FR
Tel: 01865 861879
Fax: 01865 861880

NACE exists solely to support the daily work of teachers providing for pupils with high ability, whilst enabling all pupils to flourish.

We are a large association of professionals. We deliver advice, training and materials on learning and teaching, leadership and management, and whole-school improvement.

We provide:

- specialist advice and information to teachers, LEAs and government agencies
- courses – some in partnership with Granada Learning Professional Development and with optional online continuing support and access to tutors
- bespoke courses and guidance delivered at your premises
- tutors to work alongside teachers in the classroom
- annual and regional conferences
- market-leading books and seminal publications
- keynote speakers for special events
- support for special projects
- national and international links

Some of our most popular courses are linked to our best-selling books and delivered by the authors. These are opportunities to really understand new strategies and how to put them into practice.

Join us – membership gives you:

- quick access to professional advice and resources
- members' website for updates and exchange of practice
- termly newsletters, with practical articles and updates
- biannual journals with more substantial articles relating research to practical strategies
- discount on courses and conferences
- access to network of members and regional groups

Visit www.nace.co.uk for lists of publications, courses, services and to join NACE.

Advancing teaching: Inspiring able learners every day

Founded in 1984

Registered Charity No. 327230

CHAPTER 1

Introduction – Some Observations of Gifted Students

When thinking about giftedness in science it is important for a science department to have a shared view of what is meant by a gifted student in science. This is because it is from here that the planning of the science curriculum for the gifted student in science can start. For science departments to start that process they need to examine the range of students and abilities and determine the characteristics common to their students and then to compare those characteristics with another department. Departments should be aware these will constitute criteria for giftedness and not give a definition of giftedness; the definition will become the focus of the policy for the school to determine which group of students the initiative is concentrating on. However as a process of determining provision the characteristics of giftedness in science is a good starting point.

In an LEA research project focused upon the characteristics of gifted students in science O'Brien (1997 subsequently updated by observations) reported there were particular characteristics observable in students. The project involved:

- classroom observation of students at work on specific styles of activities in science;
- teacher and pupil interviews to determine individuals' perception of science; and
- the use of logbooks to record students' ability to know about their own learning skills.

The student comments from interviews and logbooks revealed much about their perceptions of the curriculum they received and on the nature of their lessons. These remarks are perhaps symptomatic of a style of teaching and amplify remarks made by many gifted students about the highly structured way they are taught science. Frequently a significant number summed up the experience by the glib comment 'science is boring'. In the majority of cases it was clear the gifted students 'feed' on the enthusiasm and excitement of the individual teacher and they are quick to comment on the most exciting teachers and the way they brought the subject to life with stories and frequently the gifted students advanced open-ended comments which resulted in discussions on the way science affects our lives.

The evidence was originally collected from around 250 students, around 150 in Key Stage 3 and 100 in Key Stage 4 in Berkshire schools, but has been subsequently added to by observation and interview material from another 200 pupils in master-classes run for Key Stage 3 and 4 students between 1999 and 2003.

It is important to note that the evidence from the logbooks for the Year 8 students in Key Stage 3 is more forthcoming in material and comment while at Year 10 in Key Stage 4, there is a diminishing return in quantity of information from students. There is some lowering of motivation in Year 10 classes and a diminishing in the capability of the Key Stage 4 student to be involved in extra-curricular work particularly in science clubs when they were run after school. This is mainly due to outside pressures on the students' time, but many still continue with masterclass activities. In the main the notes in the logbooks are a mixture of jottings and narratives with a few diagrams. Where there are diagrams they are very representative of school convention drawings, illustrating the majority of the gifted science students in the sample are more verbally orientated.

Year 8 student observations

From the student logbooks on learning science, clear, concise and precise entries are made, many in a conversational style, almost a dialogue between student and observer. The subject matter of the work is a re-working of school class work recorded in a matter-of-fact style with many comments on the lack of difficulty they experience in the work. Often they use the logbook as a diversion to think through a self-generated problem for themselves: for example one student, in a topic on motion of objects, discusses the movement of objects spinning around the Earth.

Using diagrams and symbols with limited word explanation, the student explores an idea concerning inertia and momentum being brought on by the meeting of a comet and goes on to speculate about the effects of the planet being slowed or accelerated by the event. The example illustrated a model of interaction of forces not observed being taught in the class at the time the student speculated on the problem.

In general the student logbooks indicate a high degree of good word use, often using the word as definitive concepts and not describing events. There is a low use of diagram or pictorial representation and when present most diagrams are school science style and show little originality in their design. Many of these students are high academic achievers.

Interestingly this observation of high use of language and low use of diagram did not match with those students observed in schools where pupils came from environments where the linguistic skills are poorly developed but the students display good cognitive skills at solving problems. In this environment, due to the influence of the teaching, the students used a high degree of concept mapping or storyboarding to record information with low use of long prose using language as a conceptual tool.

Students are aware of the implications of the material for their learning towards examinations but some are critical of the relevance of the work in class to the everyday world and their lives. They are quick to make decisions about the work they consider important and that they consider irrelevant in both content and style. In general they are making decisions about what is important to them and those adjusted to the examination culture learn the facts and concepts to pass the examinations; many comment on the difference between 'school' science and 'real' science.

The logbook entries display a high level of thinking about science concepts in relation to what the student experiences outside the classroom. They display the ability to link ideas from their learning in all areas to explain events around them. The students consider this 'bridging' of concepts important and they will frequently use ideas from differing subjects to develop their thinking; this lateral nature to their work is what makes it stand out from the rest.

When given the opportunity and freedom they can construct analogous models often based upon personal experience but showing a direct, concrete relationship to the thing they are explaining. Also they use and develop taught abstract ideas such as the particle model but many are limited in their ability to use mathematics because the teacher's perception is that the taught mathematics skills are not in line with the students' demand in science.

When faced with a problem they are capable of forming longer chains of reasoning than the average student in their group. In that reasoning they show a better inferential application of science ideas rather than experiential cause and effect, leading to fewer misconceptions, and those they do harbour are generally due to poorly constructed models. This is heavily reliant upon the learnt science ideas. Many use learnt models in unfamiliar situations with relative ease: for example a student used the idea of molecules linked to each other like a ball of tangled elastic bands to explain stretching and bouncing in a rubber ball. The use of models seems to be a useful step in helping them to evaluate their investigations by allowing them to link results to a model by inductive thought.

They are quick to spot quantitative patterns and when taught about mathematical patterns they can spot quantifiable relationships between variables both in the planning of an investigation and in the analysis of results. They are fascinated by accuracy and strive to be precise sometimes to the full range of decimal places! However when the principles of estimating are discussed with them many realise the need for estimation over accuracy so they round up or down when appropriate. When measuring they match appropriate measurement scales but find the choice of range an area of challenge and this frequently leads to much discussion in practical work.

Many are confident in using accurate science language. In discussions these gifted students are fascinated with words and actually enjoy experimenting with words to describe things with a similar effect. In the development of this language much has to be said about their choice of reading and television programme. Many read newspapers, populist science magazines and watch science programmes. They form opinions and state them forcefully with much science fact but these are frequently naïve-received statements. Others have formed reasoned statements indicating something of the moral dilemmas facing the solution of science issues. For most of them populist science, as portrayed on television or in magazines, is much more interesting than school science. They enjoy the concepts of science fiction programmes like *X Files* or space exploration stories like *Star Trek* but are quick to criticise if it is not believable, hence when reading they tend to prefer science fiction to science fantasy.

There are a significant number of pupils who display high cognitive reasoning but are poor users of language who gain much from television programmes with high graphics and visual symbolism. They can be very good spoken communicators but poor written communicators and do not enjoy working with textbooks with high density of text. They will often find the curriculum 16–19 very demanding and need much input by group work and discussion.

There is often less extra-curricular activity than seen at earlier age groups but where there are opportunities many gifted students are interested in applying their science ideas to solve problems. They often attend science clubs in which they can think freely about science ideas. Some of them enjoy taking part in science awards and masterclasses but few schools in the study offer the opportunity.

When on a field visit or lecture they show great interest and challenge the experts by asking lots of 'Why' and 'What if' questions that show a degree of deep thinking, well beyond their age. They are excited by the sense of application of science and desire time to think for themselves. Some even complain that school science does not allow them to think for themselves because all the ideas are given to them and all they have to do is to learn and link them to answer questions.

Year 10 student observations

There are many similarities between the Year 8 and Year 10 students but with incremental developments in their thinking and learning skills.

The majority of Year 10 students are strongly aware of words and use language as a conceptual tool to build word models and experiment with words in a descriptive way. Sadly some of the more able cognitive students who experience difficulties with language often drop out through frustration at this stage unless they receive strong support to enable them to continue to develop their written skills. They are comfortable using symbols and mathematical applications but are often frustrated in their efforts by the limited application of mathematics in science. Diagrams often give way to written work but it is difficult to determine if this is because most schoolwork is produced in written form and their perception is that all science should be in written form. The few diagrams seen are direct repeats of school diagrams and often stylised into conventional forms.

It is very clear many of these students gain great excitement from popular and leading edge science, for example in one group there was high discussion about zero-point energy and in another group in discussion with an astrophysicist they enjoyed linking string theory, wormholes in space and black holes.

When problem solving they search for ideas from a number of contexts and sources, and link them by reference to the content or concept and not by the context and this allows them to think laterally and apply ideas. Many students comment that GCSE Science did not give them the time they wished to think widely and the school work is often easy but a lot of copying and book writing that makes it hard to go off the topic and have fun with ideas. Many also comment that the writing is always the same, straightforward notes about science and reports on practical work.

They enjoy using models, both learnt paradigm models like kinetic theory and molecular collisions, and models they have designed for themselves. For example a group of girls used an analogous idea to explain coupled pendulums as being like two people on a trampoline with one jumping and the other standing still but picking up the transferred energy and so moving up and down.

In their problem solving they are fascinated by exactness but many question the meaning of accuracy and talk about errors and the source of errors. Multivariable relationship is another area of fascination and they are capable of discussing the need to control variables but realise the limitations of controlling all variables especially in biology. For example one girl in a biology lesson comments on the difficulty of making an objective observation of osmosis when all the cells in a potato slice are different.

Students show a developing deductive logic in forming solutions and when evaluating show a concern for optimum conditions rather than an absolute sense of science proving things. It is clear they use longer chains of reasoning and a bridging of ideas from other areas to influence their thinking.

Many of these students are very critical of the science taught to them in school. They indicate that they wish to get through the examinations and recognise the need to be taught science facts but are critical of the over-structuring and many use the words 'boring' and 'limited' to describe school science. They reflect upon the nature of what they are learning and the fact that it is for an examination.

A few go regularly to a science club but this is not so prevalent as with younger students. Most clubs on offer, however, are of a revision style. Where these students attend science clubs that allow them free rein to work on science, they are more appreciative of the excitement and joy of doing science and this can be the difference in maintaining an interest in continuing with science as a subject at 16–19.

Even though those who only attend science lessons but no science clubs, respect the view that examinations are important, they are often adamant that science is not a subject that excites them enough to take further at 16–19. The difference here is made by the nature of the teacher. Keen enthusiastic teachers tend to maintain loyalty from the students and solicit a high degree of supplementary interest because of their preparedness to go outside the constraints of the syllabus in the lesson and use odd stories or extension work to excite the students.

With regard to extra-curricular activities, they enjoy watching television programmes of science content and most enjoy science fiction programmes. A majority take a science-orientated magazine; this is often set up by the school who can offer magazines like *New Scientist* at student rates and in the best situations they use articles in the lesson so there is a direct link with the outside world. In many other cases this is supplemented by a 'graffiti board' where students can bring in newspaper articles on science to display. Again the key here is the teacher's ability and preparedness to use these in the lesson often by keeping them as a cuttings book.

Concluding observation on the research

These observations indicate some of the main characteristics one can see in the gifted student but they also display some of the difficulties in teaching the gifted student. They are important to departments because, as Woolnough (1994) indicated, the critical factors in developing high levels of motivation and securing high levels of attainment for the gifted science student have been shown to be a mixture of two important things:

- a varied and exciting science curriculum through which science ideas and creativity are developed;
- the effective use of enrichment of the gifted science student's experience by extra-curricular activities.

Any department wanting to develop a high level of commitment needs to ensure there are effective structures to allow students and teachers to work on activities that are both developing and taking the science work beyond the National Curriculum for science.

With this provision the gifted science students are able to pick up knowledge quickly but it is important to accept that some will continue to experience difficulty when the approach depends mainly upon the use of text material, so there is a need for a varied diet.

They will need encouragement to learn to develop strategies to solve problems by the lateral use of ideas from widespread subjects but teachers need to remember that many will display, either overtly or covertly, a frustration with the highly structured nature of school science to pass examinations. Summarising the above material helps teachers to identify criteria for giftedness in science and to plan a curriculum to support the gifted student.

Summary of criteria for giftedness in science

Gifted students in science frequently display the following abilities. They:

- are capable of concentrating effort and attention upon reaching a specific goal, outcome or purpose and sometimes upon a specific task for a long time;
- recognise patterns and relationships in science data and link them to a conclusion by relating the change to interactions between the variables;
- make good use of specific science subject vocabulary, frequently beyond that of other pupils of their age. Words are used as modelling devices, part of the way they create abstract ideas;
- can process complex data and information quickly and can learn to mathematically model ideas, spot inconsistencies and inaccuracies in the science knowledge and discuss the occurrence of errors so they can evaluate the evidence supporting any conclusion;
- can filter out the relevant science data when presented with a lot of information;
- can form scientific hypotheses and make predictions supported by science knowledge, illustrating an understanding of the principles using relevant evidence;
- continually test ideas and make critical evaluation of the outcome to support a prediction and form a scientific conclusion;
- use new science ideas very quickly and frequently make links between differing areas of science. This makes them good at solving problems;
- have a good memory for general science ideas and principles enabling them to form models to scientifically explain situations and events;
- are very aware of the way the context affects the way the science content affects the difficulty of solving a problem. They frequently identify a personal role to help them focus on the task in solving a problem. They will make use of the context and role to create an interest for themselves. This often means they enjoy a cross-curricular approach to learning;
- are prepared to try different science ideas and novel alternative modelling approaches to solve a problem;
- may demonstrate a dreaminess or withdrawn approach to life. Sometimes this is a reflection activity allowing them time to deal with a difficult problem while thinking on something else;
- show a deep interest in science thinking problems and using reasoning skills to logically find out about things by solving science problems or puzzles;
- may demonstrate extremes of unacceptable behaviour in practical science situations because of frustration as a consequence of uninteresting schoolwork, too structured an approach, or lack of challenge in the work. This frustration can be demonstrated as an aggressive attitude towards staff but they can and do excel and persevere at self-chosen activities to produce a high standard of work, creating for some staff a dilemma;
- demonstrate a perfection in completing thinking aspects of science work which can mean they are not always the fastest but are more methodical workers in the class;
- use very creative ideas, often linking science concepts from areas not studied in school science, to embellish the work.

Therefore the main strategies a department can develop to support the gifted science students are as follows:

Strategies to support gifted science students

- **Differentiation** of classroom work to meet the needs and abilities of all in the group by varying activities or differing identified outcomes;
- **Higher Level Cognitive** or thinking **skills** and the ability to play thought experiments or build models to explain phenomena and events;
- **Extension** by going deeper into the developing conceptual models which will involve differing starting points for different abilities;
- **Enrichment** of the curriculum using different contexts or developing communication, numeracy, ICT or interpersonal skills;
- **Acceleration** by moving the curriculum on and allowing some students to complete aspects of the curriculum before their chronological peers.

Effective differentiation relies heavily on:

- clear focused objectives linked to a series of progressive learning outcomes that allow for creative and critical thinking; and
- a matching of learning styles which allow students to develop their own learning skills.

Extending the curriculum can lead to management problems unless there are coordinating structures to relate the differing parts of the science curriculum, such as careful mapping of the curriculum to ensure continuity and progression. One of the most effective ways to extend is to deal with generalised concepts and models. The student develops a greater awareness of the conceptual model and gains a growing confidence in handling and using ideas. In this model the students will extend their knowledge and understanding as a result of need rather than of direct teaching.

Many schools are reluctant to accelerate students in subjects other than mathematics. The argument is that mathematics is easier to plan for because it has a clearer hierarchical and progressive structure, making it easy to determine separate activities to allow students to work at a higher level than other peer students. It is also considered, in some circumstances, undesirable for younger students to be in a group with students of an older age because of their emotional immaturity.

A more prevalent solution to manage differing abilities is for subjects to set. This allows groups of students with similar ability levels to work together. This approach lessens the management of a mixed ability group and can ensure the students have work more closely matched to their ability. However in some schools this does not work effectively since the department does not assume differing and higher starting points in the curriculum for students. Schools tend to make groupings too rigid and not use the flexibility for occasional differing grouping such as by ability, friendship etc.

Context enrichment can be more effective for the teacher teaching in a mixed ability class situation so common at Key Stage 3, since it aims to support and promote higher level thinking. This approach does rely heavily on access to a range of resources and requires careful planning, relating specific objectives to the development of a range of mental skills. This will entail breadth to be developed in the context to challenge the student within a range of situations that can become more unfamiliar and require a higher level of thinking and degree of creativity. As the students become more successful, they learn to be more independent and want to select the content for themselves. With this independence and responsibility for their learning must go the development of sustained concentration and perseverance to complete the task and continue with an interest in science.

Context enrichment is concerned with context, communication, thinking skills and an emphasis on processes.

Context enrichment

Context enrichment is an approach that seeks to:

- give a broadening and deepening of the learning experience by considering and placing emphasis on the process of learning rather than developing content depth;
- provide experiences and activities beyond the regular school curriculum;
- develop the full potential of the student by developing their skills to use thinking in many different contexts – bridging skills;
- place emphasis on the development of creative and critical thinking;
- give breadth to the curriculum to explore areas of knowledge not generally within the scope of the common curriculum;
- develop skills of thinking which greatly facilitate the ability to solve problems and understand basic principles to enable the student to formulate models and make generalisations.

Discussion within a school on the provision for the gifted science student acknowledges the need for a department to plan and develop four areas often at the same time.

The first and most important area for consideration is the development of the classroom environment of science through the organisation of the scheme of work. Since Key Stage 3 sciences are frequently taught by teachers working in all three disciplines it is important that the scheme gives adequate guidance for non-specialists to be able to teach effectively. This should identify the organisation of thinking skills with the enquiry skills and content of the subject and development of the subject by the use of extension and context enrichment within the classroom activities for students.

Secondly the department needs to focus on the management issues of groupings, resources and definition of science abilities to allow the identification of the gifted science student.

The third consideration for the department is to ensure they have effective assessment and recording procedures to enable the senior management, coordinators and teacher to track the progression of the gifted students and make some judgement about the rate and quality of that progression.

Lastly the department needs to consider the extra-curricular provision for the student to engender excitement and encouragement. These ideas can be summarised in the Berkshire model (Figure 1.1).

Management issues		
Teacher–student interaction-groupings	Challenging materials information handling	Scientific abilities identification
Schemes of work issues		
Extension by use of graded learning objectives – relating to models, concepts, generalised ideas, process skills	Context enrichment by the use of language, differing genres, cross-curricular contexts, group work	Higher order thinking skills and use of ICT within the areas of science enquiry, problem solving and the content
Assessment of attainment and monitoring of progress		
Use of diagnostic, formative and summative assessment	Wide range of forms of assessment linked to differing aspects of science	Recording and monitoring the progress of students
Enrichment by extra-curricular provision		
Masterclasses	Contact with experts	Competitions

Figure 1.1 The Berkshire model (O'Brien 1977)

The Berkshire planning model allows the science department to link into a whole-school Gifted and Talented policy to enable the department to define giftedness in science and then through the procedures to provide structures for identification, provision, assessment, monitoring and evaluation of impact. This should set the aims for the gifted programme in science to be as follows.

Aims for the programme for gifted science students

- The acquisition of higher order thinking skills;
- The acquisition of more abstract concepts and ideas and use of mathematics as a tool to aid modelling systems and events;
- A lesson structure to allow students more time for creative thinking and reflection;
- A variety of contexts to give challenge by broadening the range of situations in which the student, having learnt the content, can apply concepts;
- Independent thinking and learning to refine the student's organisation skills;
- Cooperative group skills to promote discussion, enhance team working and use the group as a teaching medium;
- Leadership skills;
- Differing approaches to allow the student opportunities to take their study beyond the mainstream school curriculum and to develop a cultural approach to learning;
- Identification of resources that will extend or enrich the curriculum of the student.

CHAPTER 2

Talk of Giftedness, Attainment and Gender

A quick examination would lead one to believe there is little concern in this area and that boys' and girls' attainment is relatively equal. However there are differences in performance at the end of Key Stage 4 GCSE Sciences between boys and girls and a similar trend exists at GCE.

Even in the 1996 Third International Mathematics and Science Study (TIMSS) (IEA 1996/7) of Year 8/9 students' performance in science displayed a small difference in performance between boys and girls for England and Scotland. Further examination of the key stage tests reveals similar small differences and examination of the 2002 Key Stage 3 results shows a small but insignificant difference in performance between girls and boys (Table 2.1).

Table 2.1 Results (percentage) of Key Stage 3 science test for 2002

	Level 5	Level 6	Level 7	Level 8
All	33	22	10	1
Boys	33	22	10	1
Girls	34	22	9	1

The reports all indicate that across the range of questions girls and boys seem to do equally well in life science and physical science settings, so there is something else at work which creates the small gender difference seen at Key Stage 4. Key Stage 3 is the preparation for Key Stage 4 so the curriculum offered at Key Stage 3 will directly affect the performance of students at Key Stage 4.

The problem of trying to determine the performance of girls and boys is that the GCSE double science figures for grades A*–C are an expression of the students' performance in a mixture of the individual sciences while the GCE results can be viewed as separate sciences. The overall GCSE performance in science in 2002 is shown in Table 2.2. These 2002 GCSE science results break down as shown in Table 2.3.

This analysis (Table 2.3) shows some small differences in performance of girls over boys (highlighted). However, with regard to the academically gifted students if we assume they will achieve an A* at GCSE and an A at GCE then examination of the proportion of candidates gaining those grades in the science subjects and the core

Table 2.2 Performance in GCSE science (including double science) for 2002

Gender	Percentage of 15 year olds attempting GCSE science	Percentage gaining grades A*–C
Male	92	46
Female	94	50

Table 2.3 Breakdown of 2002 GCSE science results

	Attempted GCSE (in thousands)			Percentage who achieved grades A*–G			Percentage who achieved grades A*–C		
Science subject	All pupils	Male	Female	All pupils	Male	Female	All pupils	Male	Female
Single award science	52	26	26	91	90	92	18	15	20
Double award science	466	232	234	98	98	98	52	50	53
Physics	39	24	15	100	100	99	90	90	89
Chemistry	39	23	16	100	100	100	90	89	91
Biological sciences	41	23	18	100	100	100	91	90	91
Other sciences	3	2	1	95	95	96	48	49	46

subjects indicates that there are only slight differences in performance at GCSE between the genders, but at GCE A Level there are greater differences. This is shown in Table 2.4 which is based upon provisional figures (chemistry was unclear at time of analysis).

Table 2.4 Comparison of attainment at GCSE and GCE for 2002 by academically gifted students

Subject	Gender	(a) % total sat GCSE	% of (a) gaining A* grade	(b) % total sat GCE	% of (b) gaining A grade
Biology	Male	1.0	13.9	6.2	19.5
	Female	0.7	17.6	8.5	22.9
English	Male	12.0	1.9	6.7	18.8
	Female	11.6	3.6	13.4	19.0
Maths	Male	12.6	3.7	10.5	35.7
	Female	12.5	3.4	5.2	39.5
Physics	Male	1.0	18.6	0.7	25.3
	Female	0.7	18.3	0.8	31.8

Another way of looking at gifted progress is to look at the entries to A Level by age since the argument would be the gifted would be entered early because they have been accelerated in their learning. This analysis is shown in Table 2.5.

Table 2.5 Numbers and ages of gifted students sitting A Level science subjects in 2002

Subject	Gender	16 year old		17 year old		18 year old		All ages	
		Candidates	% Success	Candidates	% Success	Candidates	% Success	Candidates	% Success
Biology	Male	221	97.7	14,629	97	1,392	89.3	16,850	95.8
	Female	321	99.4	24,293	97.8	1,931	91.4	27,519	96.9
Chemistry	Male	266	98.5	13,607	98.2	1,271	93.9	15,648	97.5
	Female	289	99.7	14,199	98.8	1,341	93.8	16,310	98.2
Physics	Male	320	98.8	18,609	97.6	1,526	90.8	20,978	96.8
	Female	146	97.9	5,467	98.6	534	92.5	6,322	97.8

It is clear that on entry, and assuming teachers will only enter those who will be successful (the figures bear this out), the girls are more successful numerically in biology, in chemistry there is only a slight majority of girls over boys and in physics the boys are more dominant than the girls. On success at each age the girls outperform the boys by an average of 1.3 per cent. This difference is not too big but does seem to indicate there are some pressures leading to a bias by gender in selection of subject.

Calculating residual figures for science and other subjects indicates that the relative degree of difficulty of GCSE double science is not overall significantly higher or lower than other subjects. However when we analyse the performance of boys compared with girls it shows a difference in performance, with girls tending to show a better progression compared with boys. Possible reasons could lie in the differences seen in the development of the attitude, cognition and metacognition of boys and styles of teaching in earlier key stages particularly Key Stage 2 and 3.

Observation in cognitive psychology in the field of gender and learning indicates there are differences in the way boys and girls prefer to learn science. Boy friendly science would focus upon analytical and mechanical approaches to systems, models, objects facts and speculation while girl friendly science focuses upon social aspects, linguistically analytical approaches and linear sequential time processes.

Another factor could be the difference in levels of literacy and confidence to use verbal skills, since girls develop literacy skills sooner than boys. Talk is generally developed in girls by age three while in boys it is age four and reading is generally started in girls by the age of four while that of boys is not generally until five years old.

With this difference in verbal development it seems reasonable to conclude that at younger ages the ability to comprehend meaning from the language would allow the girls to respond well and develop conceptual knowledge in early science. At the same time boys would respond well to practical and hands-on approaches and so be more able in a science enquiry approach with relation to observation and collection of data.

The effect of this verbal advantage at this age would be to develop in girls a better confidence to deal with language in science as a conceptual tool and be more social in their approaches. The earlier start for girls might be just the edge they need to develop the faster progression seen later in the science examinations where verbal reasoning ability is so important to access and argue conceptually. The difference in physics may be its heavy reliance upon symbols, mechanical approaches and mathematical principles to develop ideas and concepts, giving boys the advantage in terms of interest but not necessarily in performance.

Within the brain there are differences that affect the efficiency in the different genders and create the need for differences in teaching. Teachers of the gifted need to be aware of this to ensure there is not a gender bias due to early advantages and teaching styles. In the brain the corpus callosum allows connections between different parts of the brain but related to the conpus callosum are the anterior commissure which is large in female brains (Allen and Gorski 1991). This allows females to tie together verbal and non-verbal information much more efficiently. A higher level of connection means communication between the hemispheres in female brains is faster allowing the brain to be able to multi-task. The slower rate of transfer in the male brain makes it more effective in separate analytical processes.

In male babies the left side of the cortex grows more slowly making the male brain more specific in its specialisation. The result of this is the male brain breaks problems down into discrete packets of information to deal with the processing. Boys find talking through a difficult problem as they work on it hard and they have generally better analytical mathematical ability, more mechanical systematic approaches to problem solving and are less happy with multi-tasking. By contrast the faster connection and less specialisation features of the female brain allow it to multi-task. Girls have the ability to talk through a difficult problem, adopt a thought-based logic approach to problem solving and have a greater general verbal ability and confidence.

At Key Stage 3 to 4 the science work starts to take on an increasingly high demand for the use of linguistic conceptual knowledge, analysis and abstract modelling skills. Boys tend to develop the logical analytical systems aspect of their thinking more favourably than girls. This could push the boys towards more speculative thinking: a mechanical practical systems approach to problem solving. Girls in the main could tend to favour a more linguistically analytical and logical thought-based approach to problem solving and favour a more social approach to science.

A number of studies over the past 20 years tend to show that, in general, in science activities there are gender differences in certain aspects of procedural understanding. Boys demonstrate a clearer understanding of the following processes and skills:

- use of graphs, tables and charts;
- use of apparatus and measuring instruments;
- speculating upon outcomes based upon trial evidence;
- interpretation of graphs and tables.

While in the area of procedural understanding the girls tend to be better in the following skills and processes:

- planning investigations;
- observation skills;
- following procedures for investigations;
- logical deductions from the evidence.

Likewise there is evidence for gender differences in aspects of the cognitive and conceptual understanding where boys seem to indicate better thinking skills in the:

- application of learnt concepts and models in physics and chemistry;
- ability to form models often involving symbols and the application of mathematical ideas in science.

While in the cognitive and conceptual understanding girls seem to indicate better thinking skills in the:

- application of concepts in biology;
- appropriate and lateral use of secondary sources to form links between ideas in science;
- linking of science work to a contextual background, particularly in using discussion to gain a greater appreciation of the circumstances surrounding an investigation.

Over the past few years there has been a good deal of work on gender differences and NfER Cognitive Ability Tests (CAT) Smith, Fernandes and Strand (2001) have found that, on aggregate, girls' ability to perform in lessons is more closely related to their measured ability. This is possibly due to a greater development of the level of metacognitive confidence influenced by their heightened confidence to use verbal reasoning.

Examination of the measured individual cognitive abilities shows girls tend to be better at verbal reasoning while boys tend to be better at non-verbal and there would appear to be general parity in quantitative reasoning. The importance to science is that to be successful in the subject the student will need a degree of parity in all three reasoning areas. For this reason science teachers need to be aware of these strengths and weaknesses and in the gifted this may be why they display a better performance, but also why they experience difficulties in certain areas of learning.

Further work on cognitive reasoning indicates many differences that seem to affect the preferences in learning style of the student. This can be seen clearly in the gifted student in science where differences in verbal skill will affect the efficiency of that student in examination situations. Generally the gifted student would be the one who scores an aggregated CAT score of 128 (personal communication with the National Centre for the Gifted Student, Warwick) but this aggregated score can disguise a varying range of reasoning skills that will affect the student in science. For this reason it is often more expedient for the school to identify those students which fit the criteria, have good attainment and are in the top 10–15 per cent of the school as gifted and then to look at those students with aggregated CAT scores of 120+ as possible candidates for the national gifted cohort. The deficiency in a student's verbal skills can be adjusted by focused intervention with literacy material in a structured higher level thinking literacy programme.

However so far it has proved difficult to develop the non-verbal reasoning skills of students with low non-verbal skills. The effect of this is that if the non-verbal is not well developed they find reasoning difficult and the transference of ideas from one area of thinking to another is more arduous for them. This programme of intervention on literacy thinking skills has implications when dealing with the planning for the gifted science student, since their giftedness in science may be more cognitive, without the fluency of linguistic skills and this will affect high academic achievement.

The difficulty for science is that at higher levels it makes use of all these cognitive ability areas and, at higher levels, both verbal and abstract quantitative reasoning become more important. What is really needed in students is a balance between these cognitive areas. Furthermore the exploitation of these skills in science to maximise potential needs careful management and planning of activities to ensure there is effective development of both gifted boys and girls.

Hence the notion that for the gifted student in science the work can be extended by making it more abstract with more use of symbols and models may advantage some students while disadvantaging others. The same can be said of extending the science by biasing the work towards more complex texts and using more secondary source work. What is required is careful diagnostic assessment of skills and then use of a balance of both approaches, focused with clear graduated learning objectives and student targets to allow the teacher to formatively assess how well the student is progressing.

When the students come to the secondary school from the primary school, social and academic differences will already have been reinforced and developed in them. Hence departments must make use of all pieces of information about their students. With respect to gender and gifted students it is important we have a carefully developed balanced programme of quantitative and qualitative assessment tools to identify a full range of skills and that these are reviewed frequently to ensure there is effective progression.

Support procedures to help gifted science students

To help the gifted science students there are a number of support procedures that can be used. Some examples are provided here.

Organisation and management of groups

In the classroom it is important to be clear about the criteria for the composition of the group and how they will work together, and also to be clear about the task and role of each individual in a group. Student preferred learning styles should be shared between departments. There is much evidence to show groups work well if they are mixed gender but balanced in numbers, with clearly indicated objectives and shared modes of working. This is very successful if it is the approach from the first week of entry into the school.

In the organisation of sets most are based upon attainment and, sometimes, behaviour. However, there may be a need to look more sharply at the records for indications of potential ability which can be used to help inform our setting arrangements and look more closely at factors affecting motivation and attitude.

In mixed ability situations there must be the opportunity from time to time to group students by ability. This allows the work to be focused for effective challenge at the correct cognitive level.

Mentors

There are three possible approaches to mentoring, each with benefits for the students. A common strategy is to link with the pastoral system by placing the responsibility on form tutors to act as the students' academic mentor and arbitrator of progress. This calls for meetings to discuss the overall progress of students but for the gifted it can act as a frequent check upon under-achievement in any subject area in relation to expected potential.

The second style of mentoring is to use other students in a 'buddy' approach. Sixth form students linked with the gifted student can be very useful in dealing with both academic challenge and shared problems of settling in to the style and culture of a school. Sixth form students can act as support in classes for the gifted and offer some challenge to them.

Thirdly we can use outside agencies and a number of schools have used PhD students or commercial scientists as mentors and support for students. For the PhD student, or the commercial scientist, it helps them to develop their general communication skills giving them the ability to explain science ideas in everyday language.

The gifted student is challenged by exposure to leading edge science and the culture of research. With respect to gender it helps to break common misconceptions about science and gender. In one school in Berkshire the use of a female physicist helped to project a more favourable attitude to physics for the girls and the following year the number of female physics students had increased by 300 per cent (increase from 4 to 16 students).

Style models

This is about making science education appear 'cool' and something worth pursuing. The engendering of an attitude and approach to science is important and this can take the form of different types of club. The use of science clubs to extend knowledge is relatively common, but there are other possibilities such as science debating clubs. Science debating clubs allow the gifted an opportunity to discuss science in a creative way.

The use of homework clubs allows the 'buddy' system to work better with closer interaction between sixth form students and other students. Another type of club seen in a school that displayed an exciting edge for the creative side of the students' thinking was the science fiction club. This focused on the use of science ideas to develop credible science stories. One centred on the idea of genetic engineering in which a human being develops a skin containing chlorophyll and is capable of producing sugar for energy.

The use of talks by smart, articulate charismatic scientists also helps to develop a style of approach that is attractive to the students. This must also include all the staff in the department. If there are charismatic teachers of science then it is important students have some exposure to them and they should be encouraged to be involved in science clubs.

Rewarding achievement

Many schools are well organised to help teachers deal with areas of difficulty but the mechanisms for rewards are often not fully developed. It has been shown by a number of schools that boys who are under-achieving can be encouraged to be more successful if their achievements are recognised, valued and in some cases rewarded appropriately.

Rewards do not have to be tangible, although there is some evidence to show that some of the more difficult students do benefit from a more tangible system at first. Letters of commendation to the student and parents can be used and private praise works just as well for many students. Certificates for achievement in masterclasses, which clearly show the objectives achieved, can be very motivating for gifted science students.

Unless the culture of the school is fully developed in an acceptance of all-round praise, the use of public praise, particularly for the boys (boys display a strong herd aspect and tend to learn in secret and play in public), can work against success since it can embarrass the student and they will then work against the system.

Dealing with under-achievement in gifted students

As always there is no one sure way to deal with under-achievement particularly with gifted students. Some will have made a conscious decision not to work because they are frustrated with something in the subject and find no satisfaction for the way they think. It is a combination of the above strategies to deal with the gifted student in science. On the whole-school level it is important that there is careful monitoring of each student's learning. This monitoring must look at the range of teaching and learning styles, the students' reaction to those differing styles and also the volume of writing they are expected to deliver in relation to the amount of listening, talking and reading. Likewise the styles and depth of reading required from students in relation to the level of comprehension expected should be monitored.

There are distinct differences in performance in relation to ability, often determined by gender and motivation, and any attempt to improve standards will inevitably have to start to concentrate on small details and look at ways to maximise efforts in lessening the detrimental effects of those differences.

CHAPTER 3

Giftedness, the Brain and Emotional Intelligence in Learning

Giftedness

Miller (1956) described humans as information processors. In his paper he argues that humans have a fixed channel capacity, in other words there is a limit to the amount of information that can be handled, processed and transmitted before it is distorted or parts of it are lost. He continues by arguing that humans construct knowledge as a result of this cognitive activity. These constructs become the personal paradigms of knowledge and may be a mixture of established models and misconceptions depending upon the way the individual constructs their knowledge. The gifted science student will be more aware of their personal constructs and some will demonstrate the ability to shift between differing constructs depending upon the problem to be solved. As science teachers it is important to be aware of the student's way of dealing with a problem to either complement or challenge the thinking.

Implicit in Miller's argument is the idea that knowledge is not a parcel that is to be delivered to the student, rather it is a thinking activity in which the students construct knowledge for themselves. However it is clear that some people are more efficient than others at handling and manipulating information and one might easily determine them as the gifted person.

Children learn to be efficient in their learning by constant practice until they become expert learners. Sternberg (1990) defines intelligence as: '. . . consisting of those mental functions purposively employed for purposes of adaptation to, and shaping and selecting of, real-world environments'. Intelligence develops as a result of learning in all environments and indeed Sternberg's definition implies a whole-world approach and the use of learning skills that employ higher mental processes in the act of thinking. To enable this to happen the learner is engaged in a dialogue with the material in which they are translating from one learning form to another; that is verbal to a model to visual to tabular to graphical.

However it is clear some students become expert learners early in their lives while others do not become experts while they are in their school years but develop the capacity to learn in later life. The question posed is: should this be and can teachers identify or find indicators for this type of student and help them become more efficient during their school years? Several sources of research show the group of gifted learners to be about 5–10 per cent of the population and those who are latent gifted learners to be another 5–10 per cent of the population. The latter is a significant proportion of the population so to help these groups would be advantageous for any school wishing to improve their overall attainment.

Greenfield (2000) identifies that the organisation of the brain is not as simple as one region involved in one specific cognitive activity and argues that an individual's affective characteristics can often influence the application of cognitive abilities and the accomplishment of a task. This makes it difficult to use simple ideas such as left-hand/right-hand brained learning. The story is more complex than that and when designing for the gifted we need to understand something of the way students learn and the way the brain is involved in learning.

Teachers know that learning is a complex mix of intellectual and emotional skills and when teachers plan the learning they rely very heavily on their personal knowledge of the student group and the dynamics that exist within that group. This gut reaction approach is often very reliable but when it comes to differentiation there is a need for more of a pedagogical approach to the planning. This is particularly true if teachers are to encourage effective independent learning. It is clear there are differences between the gifted students and the rest, and this difference is not a clear division between intellect and social skills but more one of cognition (the ability to think and reason) and of metacognition (the ability to know about and evaluate one's learning skills).

Fairbrother (2000), who made a study of students' independent learning in science, observed that there is a clear link between affective characteristics and cognitive skills. He argues that for students to become successful and effective learners they need to develop self-regulating skills in the following three areas:

- **Cognitive (being able to think)** – These are the processes that activate, guide and control our learning. Cognition is our ability to survive in the learning environment by thinking, reasoning, sorting and determining ambiguities in concepts. It assists the learning of the content of the subject, the selection of information from appropriate sources, the analysis, organisation and addition of new information and then the evaluation of and revision of one's ideas using that information.
- **Metacognition (thinking about thinking)** – This is the process of learning in which the student uses planning, regulating and evaluative strategies to think about how they should and what they need to learn. It is our ability to make reliable decisions about what is important to learn, having a knowledge of how to learn and how to use one's own skills to learn.
- **Motivation (thinking about one's confidence)** – This is the process of making decisions about one's self, how the learning will affect us, learning to take responsibility and become an independent learner. It is the ability to become a risk-taker in the learning environment. This requires the student to have confidence in their ability to use their cognitive skills and have a positive belief in her- or himself to succeed. This is the area of emotional intelligence.

Fairbrother cites, for example, the use of **concept mapping** to make sense of the relationships between concepts – this is a **cognitive strategy**. If the teacher moves on to use **discussions** about the concept maps with students in small groups and asks them to **brainstorm ideas** or solutions about a problem using the information they have, they would then be using a **metacognitive strategy**. This is because it involves making valued judgements on the learning being undertaken. If the teacher elects to set the scene and facilitate the above so the students work **independently to research** for themselves they are showing high levels of confidence and responsibility that is a **motivational strategy** and an expression of high emotional intelligence in one's learning ability.

Gifted students may have high cognitive skills and highly developed metacognition but if the emotional intelligence is not secure they will find taking responsibility difficult even though they can work independently on a teacher-structured task. It has been shown in recent work by O'Brien (2002) on reasoning skills that a student's confidence to learn is highly reliant upon their literacy skills since it is through the literacy skills that they gain access to the curriculum. In gifted students that come from inner-city or poor backgrounds, where experiences to develop language are limited, there is often a diminished verbal fluency that can affect their confidence, but their problem-solving skills can be well developed and it is frequently in science that this student will present their giftedness.

The importance of this distinction in the use of differing activities is that high achievers make use of cognitive and metacognitive strategies in their own learning. Those who are gifted and confident learners go on to develop a high intellect with good cognitive skills while low achievers may lack suitable cognitive skills, have poor metacognitive abilities or low levels of emotional intelligence and these will contribute to poor motivation. Any planning for the gifted student must consider all these aspects of learning in the school or subject curriculum. It must also consider the fact that the universally gifted student is rare and so teachers must accommodate differences and needs even in the gifted student. In science this might go so far as being better in one science than in another!

The above factors of giftedness relate closely to Renzulli's (1978) definition of a gifted student as an individual who displays above average or high levels of intellect, creativity in the forms of a fluency or flexibility of understanding of the subject demonstrated in originality of thought, and task commitment shown as perseverance, ability to apply ideas and high self-confidence in the subject (Figure 3.1).

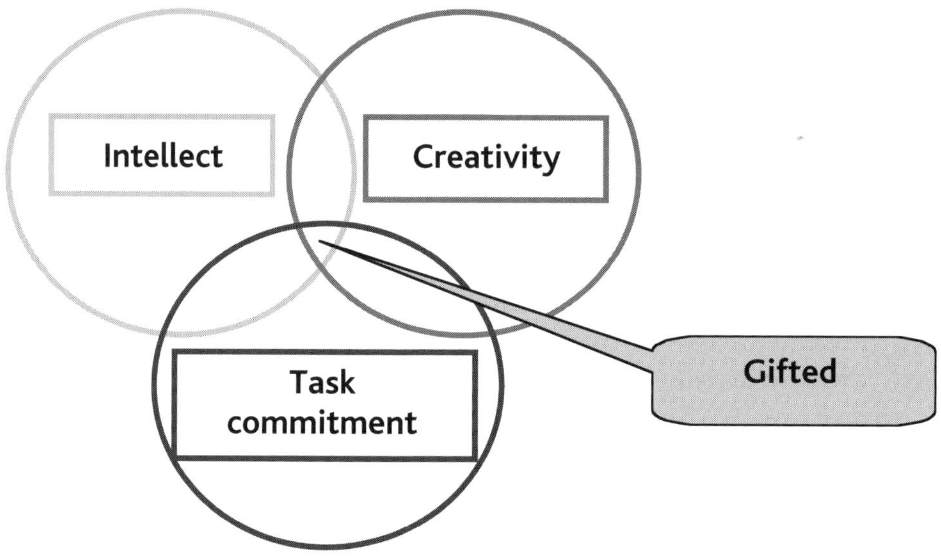

Figure 3.1 Renzulli's model of a gifted student (Renzulli 1978)

Sternberg adjusts the emphasis on intellect to argue that it is better to concentrate on cognition since intellect is a system of valued domains. Sternberg (1986) goes on to suggest that it is better to interpret intelligence as the ability to adapt to, shape and select environments to accomplish one's goals. The successful individual balances adaptation, shaping and selection, hence the successful academic student is the one who can capitalise on their strengths to attain high in those tests. Sternberg identifies three aspects of ability in an individual's intelligence and, although all of the following have to be present to demonstrate intelligence, they will be present in varying degrees to reflect differences. For Sternberg the gifted are those who display high levels of:

- Analytical ability – the ability to analyse the problem, define the nature of the problem, evaluate the options and determine a strategy to solve the problem;
- Creative ability – the ability to generate solutions;
- Practical ability – the ability to implement the options for solving the problem and make them work.

Sternberg's contention is that the differences in giftedness are attributable to differing levels in the development of these abilities and that variability will produce a multidimensional person. This would imply the abilities are domain-specific and hence the gifted science student will display giftedness in varying degrees in the domains of science and they would be perceived as being good at physics but not so good in biology. Winner (1996) sums up this multidimensional view in the following statement: 'Unevenness is the rule among academically gifted children while globally gifted... is the exception.' However, Sternberg goes on to indicate that the level of a student's performance in a subject will be dependent upon the style of teaching approach and how well it matches the pattern of the student's abilities. This match between learning style and teaching style is important.

Sternberg argues that because cognition is a fluid thing the individual will move the emphasis from one area of ability to another to develop knowledge about something. The gifted student, because of their metacognition, can easily accomplish this, giving them the ability to reason and transfer learning skills, and this is one of the qualities that determines them as gifted students.

This sense of fluid cognition closely relates to the work of Vernon (1961) and Catterell (1987) in which they argue that in the learning environment the learner uses fluid reasoning skills to develop crystallised knowledge or intellect. The gifted student has well developed general inductive and deductive reasoning skills that allow them to infer. These reasoning skills are specific to a range of cognitive domains, such as verbal quantitative and non-verbal reasoning, and include the ability to:

- acquire, organise, remember and recall information;
- detect relationships;
- generalise, transfer and use previous instruction and experience to learn new tasks or to solve novel problems;
- form and elaborate concepts;
- adapt or invent strategies and tactics as the difficulty and complexity of learning tasks or problems increase;
- monitor, evaluate and adapt cognitive processes.

Any science teacher will recognise these cognitive skills as the basis of science enquiry skills. These cognitive skills change with chronological age and with more schooling. The overall reasoning skill of a pupil will be a combination of all the cognitive skills in differing quantities since in any task the pupil works with different centres of the brain for cognition and with differing strengths in their reasoning and analytical skills.

How the brain is involved in learning

Over the past 10–15 years modern research has revealed around 80 per cent of all that we know about the brain and learning. That research has linked a number of connections between aspects of brain development and teaching styles. It would seem reasonable to consider that, since the brain is the organ used for cognitive work then its development must affect the learning potential and that the gifted learner must have a well developed brain.

The human brain weighs about 7.8 kg and is made up of 78% water, 10% fat and 8% protein and is a reddish-grey brown 'blancmange' but when dead it is pure white because of the fatty myelin insulating the axons. The largest part of the brain is the cerebrum and this part is responsible for higher order thinking and decision-making functions. This is made up of two sorts of cells. The first are called glial cells (Greek – glue). They have no cell body and are responsible for a number of functions, such as production of myelin for the axons, transport of nutrients, regulating immune systems and support for blood flow in the brain. The second are the neurons (Greek – bowstring). These are cells with many fibres called dendrites and an axon and they carry information in the form of electrical signals (nerve impulses). Each neuron generally has only one axon but many dendrites (Figure 3.2) that make contact with axons of other neurons via a junction called a synapse.

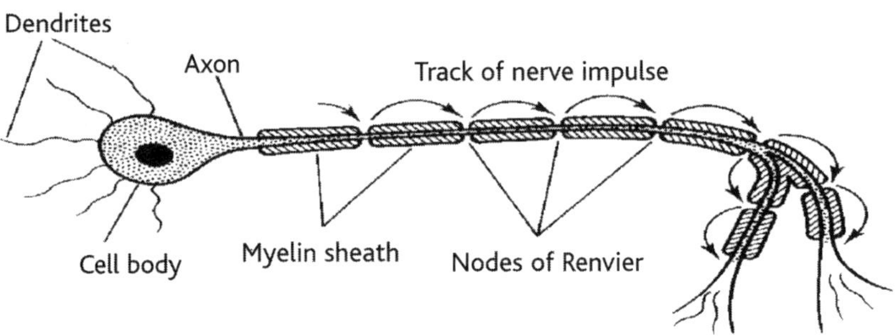

Figure 3.2 A neuron (Green 1994)

As a process, learning begins at a cellular level with the neuron processing information by converting chemical signals into electrical messages. Passing down the axon to the synapse the electrical messages are reconverted into chemical signals to pass over the gap and cause an electrical signal to be created in the next axon. Elliot (1997) reported that research indicated that when a young human baby is born it has a complement of neurons. To be effective they need to be connected to allow them to 'talk' to each other.

The dendrites or treelike branches of one neuron (see Figure 3.2) are almost touching the dendrites from another neuron at a junction called the synapse. Into this synaptic space are released neurotransmitters that drift across the gap in one direction only. This one-way flow creates 'upstream' and 'downstream' neurons as the basic units of processing. Some neurotransmitters inhibit while others excite so creating a dynamic transmission system. Calvin (1996) pictures a neuron as shown in Figure 3.3.

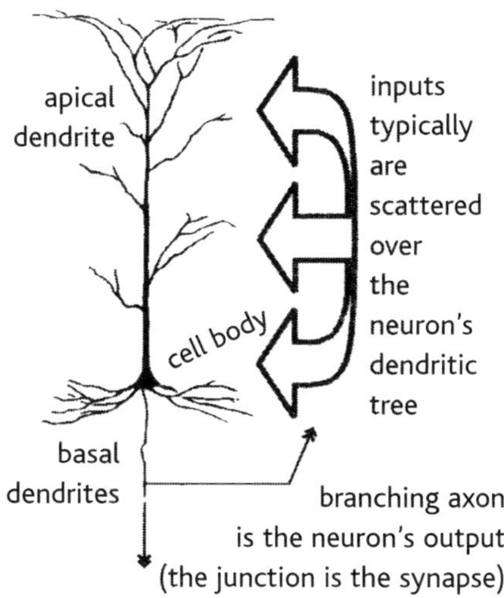

Figure 3.3 A neuron as pictured by Calvin (1996)

Calvin goes on to identify the cerebral cortex of the brain as a Darwinian machine. In the first years of life outside the womb the dendrites make many connections and any excess or connections not frequently used are removed. It has recently been shown dendrite links can be remade by focused teaching activities such as in stroke victims. Networks of dendrite communication are created during learning by such activities as repeated actions, imitation, frequent experience and problem solving. These networks are also destroyed if not used frequently.

Learning can be defined as the development and establishing of new networks of neurons. The brain of a learner is shaped by inheritance through the genes and by the influence of the environment. Jensen (1995) discusses the importance of brain-based learning and the factors that influence our own ability to learn and continue learning. He identifies these factors as:

- Genetic – the intelligence that is inherited from the parents and is marked by the efficiency by which the individual processes information;
- Nutrition – a healthy diet and balanced nutrition affects the development of the brain and this includes the fluid balance;
- Experience – the level of stimulation from the surroundings which will influence the ability of the individual to use reasoning skills and use that reasoning to interpret the world around them and construct knowledge;
- Peers – the influence of our peers on the individual's perception of the culture and way it influences how they think and the importance they place on domains of knowledge;

- Emotional intelligence – the perception the individual has of themselves and how that affects their motivation and self-esteem.

Variations in these factors can result in stress or enjoyment and the balance between stress and enjoyment is reflected in the way our brains work in order for us to learn. Figure 3.4 shows the main regions of the brain and gives an indication of just how they impinge on the ability to learn and the things a teacher can do to improve the learning experiences of the student.

It is interesting to note the similarities between the development of the parts of the brain and the identified factors that make someone a gifted learner. It could be argued that the giftedness of an individual is the result of good brain development through inheritance and favourable environmental factors and further encouragement of giftedness should nurture those conditions that promote good learning. Brain based learning has begun to address the link between physiology of the brain, the neural processing and the physical well-being of the individual.

Brain related learning illustrates that for the gifted there is an increased need to consider the variety, level and style of work being given to the gifted student. The implications are that if it is not demanding enough the individual will not develop effective learning structures in their brain. In fact it can lead to frustration in the individual and a desire to look for alternative approaches. Teachers teaching gifted students in a highly structured curriculum have frequently commented upon this characteristic.

The nature of intelligence and thinking is summarised by Perkins (1995) in his theory of intelligence, which links neural, experiential and reflective as different aspects. The neurological aspect would indicate that some students have well developed systems and are 'wired-up' very efficiently to allow faster processing, while others have faulty systems leading to inefficiencies in their learning and this aspect may well be genetic. Experiential aspects of intelligence are concerned with learning from the experience of the world and relating that learning directly to the development of reasoning to 'crystallise' knowledge into domains. This construction of knowledge allows the individual to create personal paradigms that either match the subject view or are misconceptions. The reflective aspects concern the use of creative and critical strategies to problem solve and are reliant upon thinking, memory and metacognition.

Emotional intelligence

In learning there is one other factor identified by Goleman (1995) and Mayer and Salovey (1997) as important in the development of effective learning and that is emotional intelligence. Emotional intelligence is defined as the ability to perceive accurately, appraise, and express emotion; the ability to access and/or generate feelings when they facilitate thought; the ability to understand emotion and emotional knowledge and the ability to regulate emotions and intellectual growth.

Emotional intelligence relates strongly to curiosity, confidence, empathy and sympathy and with the successful execution of an activity to a conclusion. In the main the gifted student will have developed a strong sense of emotional intelligence but not necessarily secured all the strategies to use that emotional intelligence. This may be the stalling point for a gifted student in science. This will mean motivation and self-esteem will not be positively projected to develop task commitment and there will be a low level of achievement.

Dendritic branching interconnections between neurons

Affected by limited learning approaches and styles of presentation.

Teachers should:

- use a variety of learning styles
- use a number of different presentation styles
- present students with many research tasks using many different approaches
- use a large number of application and synthesis styles of learning
- encourage modelling of ideas

Results

- better capacity for processing information
- more flexibility of thinking and ability to synthesise
- better lateral translation of ideas and thinking
- better modelling skills

Blood flow through corpus callosum

Affected by stress, anxiety, tension and fear.

Teachers should:

- create a positive, productive, exciting and thought provoking environment
- use tension reducing techniques

Results

- better learning of abstract and high level concepts
- more efficient links between different parts of the brain making thinking faster
- better retention of concepts

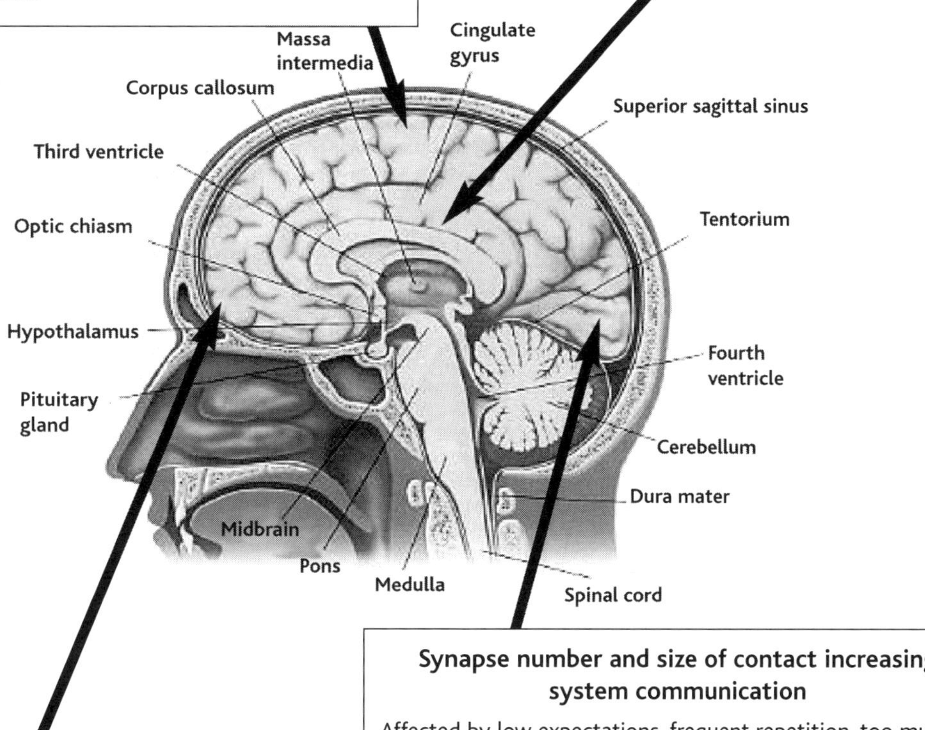

Synapse number and size of contact increasing system communication

Affected by low expectations, frequent repetition, too much support, little opportunity for independence, and poor use of social interaction

Teachers should:

- determine starting points for learning; set high expectations
- structure time and use it as a pacing tool
- use a good amount of peer teaching and social interaction with close mentoring
- use targeted and flexible groups

Results

- accelerated thought and learning
- better language and comprehension
- better processing of information
- better spatial and visual ability

More use of prefrontal cortex of the brain

Affected by high use of closed factual questions, low use of imagination and creativity.

Teachers should:

- ask many open-ended questions such as 'what will happen' and 'what if'
- use thought experiments and thinking exercises
- ask the student to evaluate their learning positively looking for future paths

Results

- high creativity
- better awareness of their learning
- more intuition

Figure 3.4 Areas of the brain that affect the ability to learn

The combination of all these elements into a programme for the gifted learner leads to the concept of problem-based learning. The learning is placed in real-life problems that are 'fuzzy' because of poor structure, ambiguity or being open ended. This creates a relevancy because the intellectual enquiry is from real life. The following example illustrates the use of problem-based learning in science.

Example of problem-based learning in science

Genetic engineering to cure disease

You are a team of scientists advising the Secretary of State for Health on the use of genetic engineering to cure disease. The dilemma you are to advise them on is should humans be cloned for the benefit of mankind?

Meet the problem

Why clone humans? Cloning would allow an infertile couple to have a child or grieving parents to replicate an individual. In 1997 scientists at the Roslin Institute transferred 277 nuclei to produce 29 sheep embryos, but only one resulted in a live birth. This demonstrated that it was possible to produce viable offspring from cloned material. The success of this experiment brought closer the possibility of replacing defective genes that give rise to genetic diseases like Parkinson's disease, sickle-cell anaemia or cystic fibrosis using genetic engineering. The hope lies in the use of stem cells taken from human bone marrow. These cells have the capability of developing into several different specialised cells. The extra embryos from fertility clinics could be another source of these stem cells. Another possible approach to the problem of these diseases is to screen for the presence of the defective genes in an individual and prevent them from or strongly advise them against having children and in this way the mutant gene will disappear from the population.

Define the problem

- Explain why genetic engineering can be beneficial or may not be worth the risks.
- Is genetic engineering a viable option for the treatment of genetic diseases?
- How might the advice session be constructed to emphasise the dangers of birth?

Gather the facts

- List what you know
  - Genetic engineering is current research and producing results.
  - Research takes time and the time scales are long.
  - The variables are difficult to control and there are many unknowns.
  - There are moral and ethical problems.
- Identify what you need to know
  - How does genetic engineering work and what are its dangers?
  - Where is research taking place?
  - What is the prognosis for success?
  - How critical is the solution of a cure for the diseases?
  - Is there any other realistic possibility to solve the problem?
- Indicate what you need to do to tackle the problem
  - Research genetic engineering using the library and Internet
  - Look for opinions from different perspectives
  - Gather data on success and alternatives
  - Evaluate success

Hypothesise

- Would a better understanding of genetic engineering help any decisions?
- Are genetic engineering or its alternatives viable?

Research and generate alternative views

Is genetic engineering or its alternatives a real solution that can be achieved in a reasonable time scale?

CHAPTER 4

Defining Thinking in the Curriculum

A thinking hierarchy

Many believe that learning is a process of collecting facts about things. To obtain those facts they often teach only the facts, organise the reading of texts, interpret diagrams and make copious notes. However, these activities do not always develop in the learner the reflective skills needed to conceptualise the information to ensure it has become embedded into their own thinking.

The above acts of learning require the relatively low level thinking skills of knowing, show knowing, apply knowing and simple analysis of information. Further, the above activities do not allow learners to acquire the **creative thinking** skills to synthesise ideas, facts, concepts, principles and processes in a new and original, or different way of using that information. They do not require **critical thinking** that is broadly reflective and centres on evaluation of how well the synthesis fits the purpose it set out to design and involves the use of skills to evaluate arguments and make judgements to inform actions needing to be taken. Essentially the student is not engaged in the metacognitive activity of thinking about how the information will affect them. In all the work with gifted students what keeps coming to the fore is Bloom's taxonomy for learning (1956):

Knowledge –	Remembering	In familiar concrete experiential situations these constitute lower level thinking skills
Comprehension –	Understanding	
Application –	Applying	
Analysis –	Analysing	In unfamiliar abstract situations these constitute higher level thinking skills
Synthesis –	Creating	
Evaluation –	Evaluating	

In recent interpretations of the taxonomy synthesis and evaluation are often translated as creative thinking and critical thinking and since both most often occur at the same time they are now shown as parallel in the hierarchy. It has also been noted that the hierarchy of thinking skills is affected by the nature of the context in which the thinking is set and the more unfamiliar or abstract, the more the student engages in higher level thinking. In the USA Resnick (1987) reported that higher order thinking skills are hard to define because they are affected so much by the context in which the student is working but they had the following characteristics. Higher order thinking:

- is not a set of routine operations; for the student the solution is not fully known in advance and they must determine an end-point, hence different groups will have differences in their solutions;
- tends to be a complex of operations and the solutions will be different depending upon different views and opinions giving rise to more than one solution;
- involves considered judgement and interpretation to determine the best fit solution;
- involves the application of differing sets of criteria which will create tensions and conflicts in the working out of solutions;
- involves uncertainty and probability in the solutions;
- is concerned with learning from one's mistakes by examination of the apparent wrongness of the solution;
- requires commitment to the completion of the task and the involvement of differing mental strategies, reflection and self-regulation in the thinking.

Kempa (1986) made use of Bloom's taxonomy and higher order thinking by developing an active interpretation of Bloom's idea. Kempa used a simple and understandable approach to learning and working with concepts and ideas by identifying the active expression of differentiating a learning task and this can be expressed in terms of science as shown in Table 4.1.

Table 4.1 Differentiating a learning task in science (adapted from Kempa 1986)

Conceptual taxonomy	Active function in the student's learning	
Knowledge – recall of facts	Student learns the language, processes, hypotheses, theories, concepts, terminology and convention of science.	Increasing levels of thinking skills ↓
Understanding of concepts	Student's ability to explain and interpret science information and express it in alternative communication modes.	
Application of concepts	Student can select relevant science information from their own knowledge to apply understanding to familiar and unfamiliar or novel science situations.	
Analysis of concepts	Students look for patterns in the data and evidence and organise the knowledge into groups or classification. In some circumstances this is mathematically modelled using graphs and statistics.	
Synthesis of concepts	Student breaks down science information into constituent parts and reconstructs the information to produce new models, knowledge paradigms or structures.	Synthesis and evaluation are equal in the hierarchy. Synthesis = creative evaluation = critical thinking
Evaluation of concepts	Student tests the information to evaluate its validity and reliability in the learning or problem-solving situation.	

What this approach indicates is learning is a complex interplay between learning the facts and understanding the concepts within the nature of the context and the style of activity demanded. An example of the use of this hierarchy for differentiation is given below.

Example of the use of hierarchy for differentiation

Teacher's notes: The variety of life – strange plants

This challenge focuses upon analysing evidence collected in the field and using that evidence to infer possible explanations. The challenge develops from the information provided on the variety of plants illustrated by two species and the differences in cell structure in different parts of any plant, e.g. leaf cell and root cell (provided in any plant biology book). Pupils will need access to a biology dictionary to interpret some of the phrases like tap root and words like chondrichthyes (= dogfish and shark family). Pupils should work in groups to analyse, reflect on and discuss the facts about the different plants and explain their reasons for their answers to the four questions asked.

Wetwitschia mirabilis (plant a) is a tree growing in the deserts of Namibia where it rains once in five years.

Rhizophora (plant b) is the mangrove tree found in many sea swamp areas, where tidal waters can surround the tree. Hence the need for stabilising branches as well as roots.

Pupils are required to draw each of the plants. This will give an indication of the skills of the pupil to interpret visual information from written descriptions. Also pupils need to appreciate that plant adaptation does not stop with the whole plant but that there is adaptation at a cellular level and that this is important when considering adaptation and variety. Finally pupils are asked to infer a further explanation for the strange behaviour of each plant during seed germination and how this behaviour is an adaptation to the conditions in which each plant lives.

Pupil challenge: The variety of life – strange plants

1. The following plants are both trees but they live in different environmental conditions. Your task is to look at all the evidence about them and decide with reasons the environmental conditions in which they live and explain how the plants have adapted to these environments. You will need access to a biology dictionary and a tape measure to get some idea of the size of the whole plant and its parts.

Plant a. *Wetwitschia mirabilis*

- Has an iron hard woody stem. This stem is about 0.75 metres above the ground and a further 2.7 metres under ground. The stem is 1.5 metres in diameter.
- It grows two long green leaves. These sprout from the stem. They grow at a rate of 15 centimetres a year and can be up to 9 metres long. In the strong winds that blow the leaves writhe on the ground where fine particles cause the leaves to tear. The torn leaf ends get tangled into a ball covering 20 square metres.
- From the stem grows a single tap root that goes down many metres. This root can store both food and water over long periods.
- The plants can be male or female but only the female can bear cones that form seeds.
- The seeds can wait up to five years before germinating. Unlike other plants the cotyledons can last for up to five years.

Plant b. *Rhizophora*

- Have long slender woody stems that grow tall. On the top are branches that grow out and up like a normal tree. The lower branches grow out and down without leaves. They act as stabilisers for the long slender stem.
- The top branches produce many small rounded evergreen leaves that form an impenetrable forest.
- The lower branches and roots form a scaffold or web of wood, which acts as a safe habitat for coelenterates, molluscs, crustaceans and chondrichthyes.
- Fruits are produced on the upper branches and seeds form inside the fruits. In the damp atmosphere of the fruit the seeds germinate and produce a single root that grows downwards for 25 centimetres. When the seed is ready it detaches from the tree and falls root downwards. The root spears the underlying surface and the root supports the seed that then continues to grow into an adult plant.

2. Draw a diagram of each of the plants labelling all the plant organs you can. See if you can model how each plant carries out all the functions of a living plant.
3. Each plant has leaves but they are different in shape and structure. Using the information from a biology textbook draw the possible leaf shape for each, a diagram of the leaf cells in cross section and explain the possible adaptations.
4. Explain why you think the two seeds have such strange germinating styles indicating how each is adapted to the different environments.

Reasoning and modelling

Reasoning plays a big role in this drama of cognition because the process results in mental models and in science the model is an integral part of the solution. Gentner and Stevens (1983) advance the view that mental models can be created by examining a system and committing the elements of the system into the long-term memory as units in a causal system. This mechanical approach is dependent upon building domains of specific knowledge. When the individual encounters a similar system they draw on this long-term memory to visualise the new system and make sense of it. Gilden and Proffitt (1989) have investigated this approach by asking candidates to observe collisions between moving and stationary balls to determine which ball is the heavier. Any judgement will require a consideration of velocity and trajectory prior to collision. Their results indicate that people make simple heuristic evaluations such as: 'The ball moving faster after the collision is lighter', or 'The ball that ricochets more is the lighter.'

Both heuristics are frequently correct so the observer gets more correct than incorrect answers but they do not fully integrate all available information to answer the question correctly on all occasions. Although this approach appears to demonstrate quantitative aspects, it is dealing with relative notions of values and so is qualitative and makes more use of visualisation skills to evaluate the system and its solution.

Gopnik and Meltzoff (1997) have explored the idea that children's thinking imitates this approach to make sense of the world and in this way they create and use theories much as scientists do to predict and interpret events. Inagaki and Hatano (1987) suggest young children develop their reasoning through mental models by forming analogies and in the biological area they can transfer the information from the biological domain and from a familiar species to an unfamiliar species to make sense of what they see.

The big difference between the scientist and the child is the child is more affected by their beliefs while the scientist is more influenced by the accepted paradigm governing the domain of knowledge. In older gifted science students it is often observed that they are more in line with the scientist by being influenced by the paradigm, hence indicating a significant difference between them and other peers.

It has also been observed that linguistic skill concerned with written text is an important instrumental tool in developing science reason in the older age range of students. This may explain why the gifted science student is more gifted since they can make use of language as a conceptual tool to discriminate.

Another function more developed in gifted science students is that of the skill of categorisation or learning how to classify. Lassaline and Murphy (1998) suggest that an individual when faced with a multitude of objects looks for structural similarities and categorises on these to form clusters of similarities, which constitute taxonomy. The distinction between the gifted science student and the average is their ability to seek and make use of differences. Again the level of linguistic development is a compromising factor for the individual and crucial for progress in science.

Once the student has formed a category, with its criteria for belonging, they are quick to make inferences based upon inductive thinking and it is the formation of generalisations that enable the gifted to reason so quickly in science.

In conclusion, reasoning is a mixture of logical deduction that operates on the level of making representations of events independent of content and so is domain-general, such as making comparisons and detecting commonalities and differences. Domain specific aspects, which involve the use of analogy, mapping and classification, are dependent upon content and context. Domain specificity will incur the use of linguistic forms as conceptual devices and so will be more difficult for the individual in thinking terms. Within the domain, concepts will be aligned by their connections. Thus in any problem the individual will test for structural consistency to verify the reasoning rule and the logic developed. This can be made use of in designing tasks that are differentiated as shown in the following example.

Example of a differentiated class activity

Darwin and the plastic turtles

The pupils are given a group of six plastic animals, say six turtles (loggerhead, leather back, deep sea, rock, etc.) belonging to the same group but different in a number of ways. They first examine for differences and similarities and then move on to draw up a key to allow someone to identify the creature.

Asking students to form a key is a relatively quick operation since they will have encountered the task at Key Stage 2. For the gifted pupil this is not really a challenge so differentiation is needed to enhance the task for them. The gifted students are told the following:

You are Charles Darwin's assistant on the *Beagle* and the sailors have brought in this array of animals found in a wide area. The ship is due to sail in two days' time.

- You have to examine the creatures and note the differences and similarities.
- From those similarities and differences you must decide if they all belong to the same group.
- From the features seen decide the environment the animal might inhabit. Explain your reasoning for Darwin so the sailors might be instructed to search those environments to see if they can find the same species again.
- From the features determine any that are adaptations to the environment and justify those adaptations.

Using reasoning skills as a differentiation tool within a context emphasises the awareness teachers need in their planning about the student's cognitive skills, the language demand, the nature of the context and the manipulative demand of the activity. The differing developments of each of these reasoning skills in gifted science students lead to the identification of different types of giftedness:

- **Academic** – These students acquire a substantial and organised body of knowledge, which they can use fluently and effectively to solve problems and make decisions about modes of action. These students actively seek out information and facts on minute detail of systems and 'know all about things'.
- **Self-determined** – These students are capable and able to acquire the tools to learn by themselves. They frequently make decisions about the importance of certain domains to themselves (as in Sherlock Holmes where he determined certain subjects, like chemistry, were essential and he made himself a foremost expert, but that astronomy served no useful purpose and so he did not bother with it).
- **Strategic or Cognitive** – These students develop a repertoire of thinking strategies which empower them to be able to learn, control and guide their own learning. These students have an abiding passion for learning and seeking connections between different domains.
- **Emphatic or Charismatic** – These students are capable of viewing the world from many different perspectives other than their own and can appreciate the differences in cultural views.

This range illustrates that there cannot be a single approach to provision and that the thinking approach to the science curriculum is the most productive since it can cater for the differences. The thinking in science should promote in-depth learning, the ability to recognise relevant from appropriate, essential from optimum and precision from estimate. The content and contexts need to be from the real world, which does not categorise thinking into a single domain but gives a holistic approach recognising the culture of the subject and the society and any clashes that there might be in the context in which the problem is placed.

Creative and critical thinking

The gifted student is well fitted for this high order creative and critical thinking curriculum but in many departments concerned with high level attainment in national tests the transmission style of teaching and learning predominates in order to cover content at the expense of the thinking. The result is that many students, including many gifted students, adopt emotive and habitual thinking processes, that is thinking based upon past practice or emotion.

The gifted students do not consider the cultural view or how new data, coupled with other evidence or facts, supports or challenges a particular viewpoint: in short they do not engage in questioning the ideas themselves. Creative and critical thinking is affected by the adoption of habitual and prejudicial thinking. Therefore one way of developing the curriculum for the gifted science student is to consider the issues and methods of science as the following example shows.

Example of considering the issues and methods of science

Galileo's dilemma: Is rolling the same as falling?

Investigate Galileo's experiment on falling bodies using an object rolling down a slope compared with Newton's idea of a falling body from a height.

Students approach the experiment as an investigation into falling bodies and start by explaining why Galileo's experiment is not a true representation of a falling body.

This investigation will help the gifted student examine how method can affect the resulting conclusions. They need to examine the nature, range and relationship of variables and the range of measurements. They will need to examine what constitutes a sensible range and accuracy for measurement. They should determine what errors there are, how they can be observed and quantified and how Galileo's experiment could be used to investigate falling bodies. It will help them to appreciate the range of errors involved in an experiment and how scientists use analogies as models. It also demonstrates that simple elegant experiments can be very useful in verifying ideas.

The experiment can be used as a discussion piece on the concepts of reliability and validity.

The constructivist view of how we learn science takes into account the interaction of creative and critical thinking that has a direct relationship to an individual's personal experiences and the patterns used to learn about the phenomena and explain events. The notion of people constructing their own meaning from experiences, teaching and concepts, implies individuality about the way individuals learn and construct reality.

Individuality in learning does not mean opposing views or unique understandings but implies consideration for the style of teaching in relation to the style of learning. It is more likely gifted students are more aware of their preferred ways of learning and because of this are able to accept alternative approaches to explain an event.

The following examples of using history as a context for creativity in science will require the students to use their ability to think and their knowledge to extend their learning.

Examples of using history as a context for creativity in science

Use an historical context to teach science ideas and examine the development of those ideas such as:

- Aristotle's evolutionary ladder compared with Darwin's idea;
- The view of the Universe from Ptolemy's time to our own time;
- The atomic model of matter versus a continuous idea of matter;
- The phlogiston idea versus oxidation as an explanation of combustion.

Let the students research the different points of view and the evidence for each viewpoint that existed at the time. Then advance opinions on why certain ideas were acceptable at a particular time and what caused ideas to change.

It is perhaps appropriate to illustrate the difference between intellect and cognition at this point, since both intellect and cognition are related to intelligence.

According to Calvin (1996), paraphasing Piaget, 'Intelligence is what you use when you don't know what to do next.' It is difficult to define intelligence and when dealing with gifted students it is easy to be confused into thinking that the solution to dealing with the curriculum is to just make the content more difficult. However this is too simplistic since it assumes the intelligence is something that can be topped up with more knowledge just like one tops up a pint of water with more water. For that reason, many, such as Richardson (1999), prefer to approach the topic of ability by not using the term intelligence, but defining cognition as the ability to use one's thinking skills to survive a learning environment. Richardson defined intellect as: 'Those skills related to knowing how to encode and decode information. Intellect is related to memory and organising and grouping knowledge into domains.' The implication of this definition is that intellect is related to the processing of information or cognition, but within the context of a discipline or body of knowledge like science, history, mathematics or art. It is within a discipline such as science that the gifted student will be identified by their teachers. Lewin (1987) makes a clear distinction between putting more emphasis on cleverness than upon wisdom, a situation in which the child learns to use their verbal fluency to construct answers to questions and not display rational use of knowledge involving critical or creative thinking to solve problems.

Lewin identifies this confusion of cognition with intellect as the intelligence trap – 'A child knows, but not how to use, an answer.' That is they know the factual answer but do not understand how to use it. He is arguing for some breadth in the curriculum for the gifted students. This can be seen as enrichment of the curriculum by the use of thinking skills within new contexts to present challenge. The following examples require relatively simple science knowledge but it is the interaction of all the parts that creates a difficult cognitive science problem.

Examples of Science thinking problems Key Stage 3

1. Describe what will happen when the tap in the middle of this device is opened so the two balloons have a fully open connection to each other?

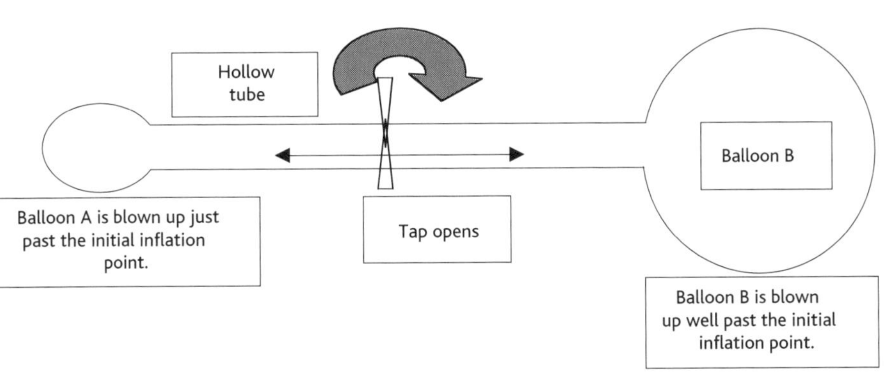

2. Describe what will happen when the candle burns at both ends? Explain why and what is causing the effect.

Candle can turn about the central point.

3. Describe what will happen to the temperature of the liquids in the two beakers when the hot plate is turned on. Explain why the temperature does what it does and what is causing the effect.

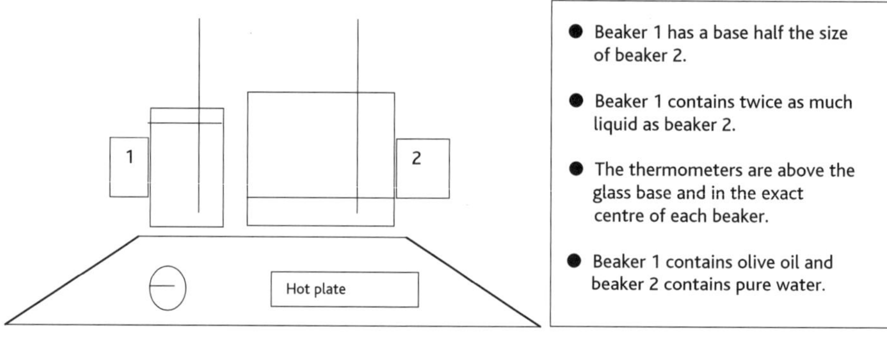

- Beaker 1 has a base half the size of beaker 2.
- Beaker 1 contains twice as much liquid as beaker 2.
- The thermometers are above the glass base and in the exact centre of each beaker.
- Beaker 1 contains olive oil and beaker 2 contains pure water.

4. Compare a golf ball and a hockey ball. Describe the differences. Explain why the golf ball has dimples and why this helps it go further than a smooth ball. Research into how this helped with an important bombing event in World War II. Does number of dimples or size make more differences? Design an investigation to find out.

5. This is connected with problem 4 above. A man working for the RAF used an idea that every school child uses when throwing a stone in the sea. By careful throwing the school child can get the stone to skim across the water's surface. This idea helped to solve a difficult problem. It may have started with throwing stones into the sea but it continued to marbles and a catapult on a Surrey common. He was only imitating an 18th century naval commander. Work out what the critical angle was and why that angle was so important for the effect.

6. Draw a diagram of the following to help you see what is happening. Two cylindrical plastic bottles are lying on their sides on the floor of a railway carriage so they can roll in the direction of travel of the carriage. One bottle is one third full of water and the other is one third full of 50:50 water and olive oil. Predict the movement of the two bottles during the journey shown in the graph. Explain your predictions for each bottle and explain any differences between the two bottles.

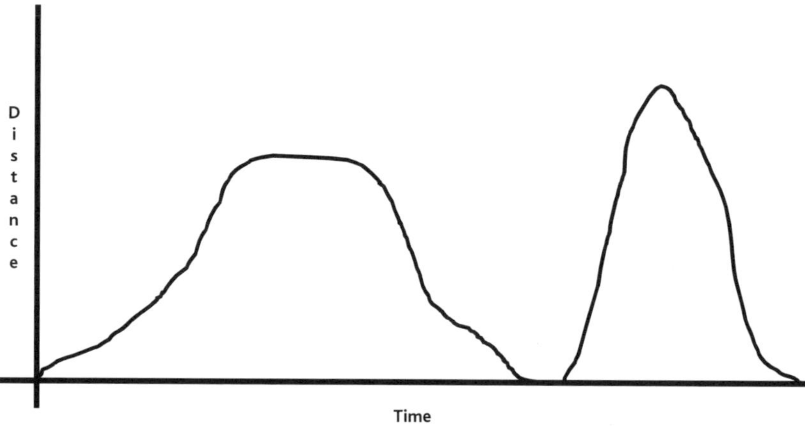

7. The Earth loses heat that is radiated from its surface but the loss of heat by radiation is different for water and soil. Water is also a very poor conductor of heat while soil is a better conductor. When pure materials form solids and liquids they change state without changing temperature the energy goes into the forming or breaking of bonds

in the material. This energy is called latent heat because it is hidden (*latent* means *hidden*). Use this information to solve the following problem:

- the latent heat of fusion of water (energy used when water freezes at 0°C) = 333 kJ per kg
- thermal conductivity of ice = 2.1 j per sec per metre per Kelvin
- density of ice = 0.92 kg per metre.

The temperature above a pond is 5°C below zero so a skin of ice forms. Below the ice layer the liquid water is slightly above freezing at 0.5°C. As the ice thickens the latent heat is transferred through the ice layer and radiated away into the evening air. This creates a very smooth layer of ice. Complete the following:

(a) The layer of ice is 20 mm thick. Estimate in mm per sec how quickly the ice is thickening if the temperature remains constant.

(b) Design an experiment to measure the rate at which ice freezes.

(c) Why does the pond not freeze totally solid?

8. Some reactions are highly exothermic (*exo* means *to give out*) and this can be used for a number of purposes such as the instant hot coffee drink containers seen at some garages. If the released heat can be transferred either fast or slow then we can use the phenomenon. Design a hand warmer and a self-heating can that can heat food to a temperature of 70°C and hold it at that temperature for 45 minutes. Calcium oxide releases 65 kJ per mol when mixed with water.

9. Predict which candle will go out first in the following experiment. Each container contains air at room temperature and is sealed to the bench with soft paraffin gel. Explain your prediction.

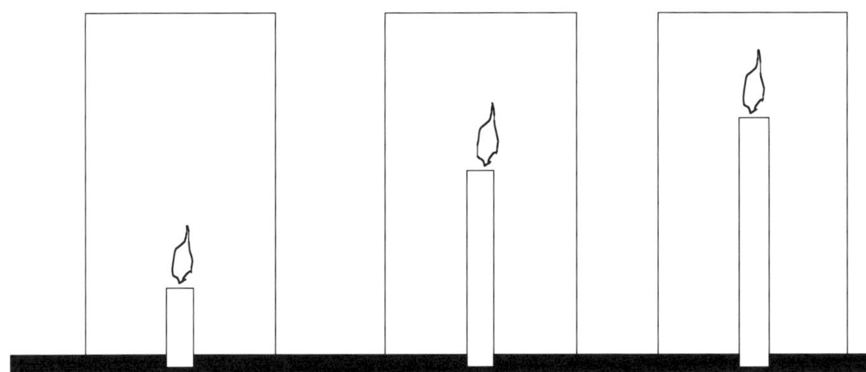

10. An acid reacts with a carbonate to release carbon dioxide; also heat on some carbonates releases carbon dioxide from the carbonate. This knowledge is used in cooking to 'raise' the food by creating small cavities of gas such as in a cake or in bread. Design a piece of apparatus to calibrate the release of gas from a series of standard amounts of acid plus carbonate.

11. A plant puts out root hairs into damp soil. These root hairs are very thin, often only one cell thick. Osmosis occurs when water moves across a selectively permeable membrane from a less concentrated solution to a more concentrated solution. The water can pass from one root cell to another by osmosis and so to the stem where it moves up a tube called the xylem to the leaves. Plants lose water from their leaves as water vapour by

transpiration. This helps to cool the plant and ensures water reaches the leaves for photosynthesis. Predict what would happen if:

(a) the temperature rose around the leaves
(b) the humidity increased around the leaves
(c) if there was no wind
(d) if the hole through which the water transpires is large or small.

Now decide how plants survive in the desert and in swampy conditions.

12. You have a litre beaker marked with graduations of 0.5 cm and it contains a litre of water at 8°C. You place a cube of solid ice straight out of the freezer into the water. The cube measures 5 x 5 x 5 centimetres and it floats with two-thirds of the ice below the surface. Predict the new level of the water in the litre beaker.

The ice is left for two hours in a room of 20°C and the ice completely melts. Now predict the new level of water in the beaker. What would be different if carbon dioxide at a temperature of –15°C was bubbled through the water for the same two hours?

13. The following table is an indication of the variation in blood groups of different ethnic groups:

	Percentage of group with blood group			
Ethnic group	A	B	AB	O
Welsh	35	10	3	52
Nigerian	21	23	4	52
American Indian	22	0	0	78
US Afro-Caribbean	27	21	4	48
US Caucasian	41	10	4	45
Indian	25	38	7	30
French	45	9	4	42
Chinese	27	23	6	44

(a) From analysis of the data what conclusions do you come to about the distribution of blood groups and any gene differences among the different ethnic groups?
(b) Explain if there is any evidence of migration of any of the ethnic groups.
(c) If there is intermarriage in approximately 10 per cent of all families of the different ethnic groups what would be the possible outcomes?

14. A ball is dropped into a hole that goes right through the Earth as in A.

Explain:

(a) what will it do?
(b) what will the ball do if it is dropped into a hole that goes through the outer part of the Earth as shown in B?

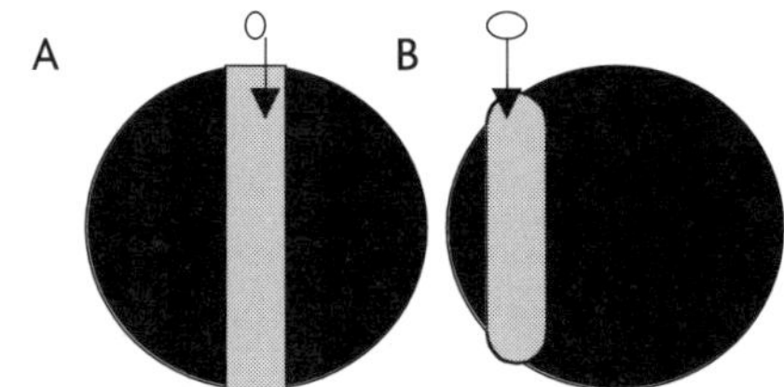

To solve the problems the student will need to use their cognition skills using the appropriate science ideas and concepts. There are a number of possible solutions but the most likely solution will only be developed by a careful examination of the interaction of all the ideas and an evaluation of the probable outcomes.

In these problem-solving contexts the individual's intelligence can be defined as the use of a complex of science intellect and cognition. That is the act of knowing science, being able to show that knowledge of science principles, taking the science principles apart to reapply them in the given context and using that knowledge to solve the problem and evaluate how well that thinking works.

Multiple intelligences

This definition of intelligence as a complex interaction between intellect and cognition makes it hard to measure intelligence within a discipline. It also means that individuals will use their intelligence to solve problems in differing ways. In Gardner's (1983) view there is not one stable measurable quality that one would call intelligence but there are a number of traits or ways of thinking that influence our learning approach. Gardner calls these thinking traits intelligences.

When looking at any problem it will be perceived within a specific environment and the context of that environment will determine a framework that will determine a trait for the thinking. This learning context will be embedded in one of the number of differing intelligences that Gardner identifies. To date Gardner has identified nine intelligence traits, sometimes referred to as the seven plus two. The seven relate to content and are as follows:

- **Verbal–Linguistic** – concerned with verbal and language. Students who excel in language studies and show excellent ability to write or talk well dominate in this intelligence trait.
- **Logical–Mathematical** – concerned with logic, systems, critical and scientific thinking. Students who are gifted in logic, mathematics and science often dominate in this intelligence trait.
- **Visual–Spatial** – visual and spatial awareness of the pictorial media. Students who demonstrate the ability to visualise and convert diagrams to tangible objects, have a good sense of direction and often with artistic talent tend to dominate in this intelligence trait.
- **Body–Kinaesthetic** – concerned with senses and movement. Students with a bias towards the arts and crafts tend to dominate in this intelligence trait.
- **Musical** – concerned with rhythm and sensitivity to sound. Students able to determine a rhythm and rhyme often dominate in this intelligence trait.
- **Environmental** – awareness of the environment and the interactions of the individual with the environment. Students with a sense of the interdependence of living things with the environment and a concern with that interdependence often dominate in this intelligence trait:
- **Moral–Ethical** – awareness of what is right and wrong. Students who show an awareness and concern with justice and morality often dominate in this intelligence trait.

The plus two relate to one's thinking with others or to one's metacognition:

- **Interpersonal** – an awareness of social interaction and working in groups. Students who show high charismatic flair, the ability to get on with people and 'gel' groups together to accomplish a goal and enjoy the experience often dominate in this intelligence trait.
- **Intrapersonal** – an awareness of inner feelings and their confidence. Students who show a high understanding of their own potential, and are able to engage in objective self-analysis and enjoy their own company dominate in this intelligence trait.

From the above list of intelligences it is possible to see how an individual will use all aspects of these intelligences to a greater or lesser degree in their learning. So in a science context it is possible a number of different individuals will use a range of intelligence traits. A teacher of the gifted science student will need to consider these traits since the individual gifted science student will be aware of their own strengths and weaknesses within their thinking.

Since these intelligences will influence the style of thinking an individual will engage in and they will be present in various levels of development they provide the science teacher with a means of differentiating a task without changing the level of content. Changing the thinking trait for the activity will present a degree of context enrichment that will in itself be a form of differentiation. Further, the individual style of thinking will be emphasised by the nature of the activity and the context in which the learning is embedded. An example is shown in Table 4.2.

Colin Rose (1985) first developed Gardner's approach of multiple intelligences into the six stages of learning. With many gifted pupils in science using this approach can give them the ability to be able to learn for themselves and become independent learners. The approach adopts the following steps:

- **Stage 1 – State of mind**: This relates to the emotions and motivation and the ability to access the work through revision and reflective thinking and to the development of long-term memory. In the science lesson it relates to the development of a positive attitude to the subject, making it exciting and getting the students to take an interest in the subject while indicating the expected outcomes and science areas to be covered.
- **Stage 2 – Intake of information**: This relates to the visual, auditory, verbal and kinaesthetic aspects of the lesson and the way the students prefer to learn. Bearing in mind students will learn in a mixture of ways the teaching of the information needs to be in a number of different forms to allow all students the opportunity to access the necessary information. For example reading about the atom, watching a video on the changing states of matter, using a computer simulation on food chains, discussing the way a body can be slowed by forces, etc. Gifted students know much about their own ways of learning and so can be conservative about the way they learn and need to be convinced about the different ways.
- **Stage 3 – Exploring the subject**: This relates to the developing of understanding by the processing, categorising and reorganising of information. For example modelling ideas or making 3D models of things like different cells; writing and acting scripts for radio or television programmes on topics like the kinetic theory; using mapping activities such as a flow cycle for the rock cycle or concept map on dissolving; contrasting a table of similarities and differences

Table 4.2 Differentiation using intelligence traits

Differentiation level	Verbal–Linguistic	Body–Kinaesthetic	Logical–Mathematical
Low	Write a science description of the way different rocks are formed from molten rocks. You must use accurate science language.	Watch the crystals form under different heat conditions. State how it is similar to the formation of rocks and record a verbal description of the changes.	Draw a concept map of the rocks and formation of rocks using the words given: magma, lava, igneous, crystal, basalt, granite, pumice, lithosphere, vent, tsunami, plate and tectonics.
	Create a time line or diary of rock particles in different types of molten lava as they form different igneous rocks.	Describe the rock cycle and place the different picture cards describing the changes in the right order.	Label the diagram of the rock cycle with the correct labels and complete the cycle so it flows in the correct order. Write a paragraph describing the order of the formation of igneous rocks.
Mid	Write a science story about the way different igneous rocks form in a volcano like Etna and the way the land changes.	Follow instructions to show the formation of crystals under different conditions and describe how this relates to the formation of different igneous rocks.	Define the following words and use them in a science report on the formation of rocks: magma, lava, igneous, crystal, basalt, granite, pumice, lithosphere, vent, tsunami, plate and tectonics.
	Write a conversation between feldspar and mica as they form igneous rocks in different conditions and the way the landforms differ because of the different rock forms.	Role-play using the cards of the rock cycle and convert the role play to a diagram showing the formation of rocks.	Learn the rock cycle and from memory draw your own rock cycle and formation of igneous rocks.
High	Devise a debate on the formation of rocks under different conditions and the possibility of predicting eruptions.	Devise and enact a play describing the formation of rocks from molten magma inside the Earth to igneous rock on the surface.	Write a case study comparison of the Mount St Helens eruption of 1980 and the Peléan eruption of 1902. Describe similarities and differences in the eruptions.

for reflection and refraction of light; composing a song, poem or rap on ecosystems; making a poster or flow chart on energy transfer and conservation; writing a diary on the life of an atom of oxygen in a piece of wood that undergoes combustion followed by photosynthesis and digestion; etc.

- **Stage 4 – Memorising the information**: This relates to the processes of redrafting and reviewing work by students and is integral to the processes used in stage 3, but average and less than average students need guidance on what the important ideas are while the gifted should be challenged to identify what they believe are the key ideas and facts.
- **Stage 5 – Show what you know**: This relates to the summative assessment of the work undertaken by the student. It does not necessarily mean the performance in an end of module test but will call for a range of assessment techniques involving teacher, peer- and self-assessment.
- **Stage 6 – Reflecting on the learning**: This relates to the metacognition of reflecting on and reviewing the learning strategies used and how successful they were for individuals and evaluating the level of learning.

The Learners' Cooperative (1996) have used Rose's model in conjunction with the idea of learning intelligences to differentiate science lessons for students with differing levels of learning skills but often with some potential to learn and as revision materials for students. The materials are a rich source of ideas for teachers on differing learning activities to both engage and excite all learners. The editors of *Science Web* (Horsfall *et al.* 2001–2003) adopted the same multi-sensory learning approach and these books have been written specifically for the middle to high ability science student at Key Stage 3 to develop both their thinking and their science knowledge.

Intelligent action has more to do with a flexible adaptation of means to reach a desired goal. This desire to complete or strong commitment to task will make use of an intellect or body of knowledge and a logical reasoned cognitive approach to problem solving. In science the impression could be that the dominant thinking trait would be logical–mathematical but it has been shown it is possible to design activities in other thinking traits or intelligences. It is important to realise these modes of thinking and endorse them in the activities offered to students in science since they can be coerced into emotive and habitual thinking processes through the repetition of the same diet of teaching.

Reasoning and learning styles

Teaching thinking involves the student in the use of reasoning skills. The information from various cognitive ability tests, such as those in Cognitive Acceleration through Science Education (CASE) or the MIDYIS test from the Centre for Educational Management at Durham or nferNelson, can provide some information on the presence and level of the reasoning skills of classification, inductive, deductive and inferential thinking allowing a basic measure of the student's capability to learn to be determined.

Confident gifted learners will show ability to take risks in the learning situation while gifted students with little or no confidence and least able learners would show the converse. The ability to use different forms of reasoning will affect the student's efficiency to think and so could affect the metacognition and motivation of the learner. A low attainer will be the student who finds it difficult to use the different forms of thinking and translate between the different activities of learning. That efficiency can be affected by strengths or weaknesses in the cognitive development of the student.

Vygotsky (1962) stressed the importance of cognition in the learner in constructing their own knowledge systems and the important role of the teacher as one that cognitively challenges the student by many different means. In his work he also indicated the importance of developing scaffolds to assist the learner.

The development of an individual's learning style will be influenced by the ease and comfort of learning in particular ways. Sternberg (1994) defines a learning style as: 'A style is a preferred way of using one's abilities. It is not in itself an ability but rather a preference,' and comments that 'Most teachers are best at teaching children who match their own styles of thinking and learning.' There is evidence that this preference in a learning style will be affected by one's confidence in dealing with reasoning skills in language, codes and symbols (namely the use of written language), diagrams, numbers and symbols. In order to use these forms effectively an individual needs to be able to develop simple rules of logic and then to apply those rules to make sense of the situation. Differences in the individual's strengths to use verbal, quantitative and non-verbal logic will affect the learning style of the individual.

The idea of using individual learning styles for teaching is not a new one – it has been extensively researched and written on. It could be argued that Feuerstein's work (Feuerstein and Hoffman 1980) on developing potential to performance is an examination of differing learning styles and in his work he has shown that all students have the capacity to learn to think. There is often a progression of process skills used for learning and in the gifted student in any subject these will show marked development in a number of areas such as:

- In their use of **language** which is often extensive with use of subject and general words outside their peer group range, very precise and often concise but showing the desire to experiment with language when describing events and phenomena or modelling ideas. They recognise words as conceptual devices and develop strong analogies to demonstrate an awareness of ideas.
- Concern with **accuracy and precision in practical work** and when discussing errors show a concern with reliability and validity when evaluating the work.
- The ability to develop both **mental and physical models** using concepts or ideas higher than their age or peer group. These models can be both analogies and their own interpretation and description of a paradigm model, application/development of more sophisticated models of their own or mathematical modelling.
- The use of graphs or **mathematical treatments** of a problem at a higher level than their peers. They use them with confidence and when taught the mathematical principles can derive relationships and correlations from those graphs. They can, when taught how, consider error mathematically and its effect upon the results.
- They demonstrate good control of their **creativity** and focus it upon a conceptual idea or skill to produce a performance that is outstanding when compared with their peers.

- They have a high awareness of their own learning characteristics and demonstrate a good **personal understanding** of their **own learning style** and the way they think – **metacognition**. This high degree of metacognition enables them to reflect upon their experiences, engage in self-criticism and evaluate learning experiences as important or not to their learning.

Content, context, reasoning and CASE in the science curriculum

Yet the mere progression of these areas needs caution when dealing with those students who are gifted in any subject. After the publication of Shayer and Adey's (1981) research on the science education content being taught to secondary students it became clear that there was a dichotomy in the science curriculum.

The majority of students were receiving a curriculum that was inappropriate for them and they were not interacting with the curriculum by thinking about the science of the subject. They were learning facts as statements of truth and not learning to think about the weight of evidence or relevance of science methodology. A minority of students, generally the more able (now called the gifted), were being challenged by problem-solving activities such as those found in the Nuffield style science courses.

The possible reason for this hierarchical approach was that formerly educationalists followed Piaget's view that, with careful teaching experiences all students would develop their cognition from concrete to formal thinking. However Shayer and Adey's work indicated that only about a third of students, generally the more able students, in British schools actually moved to formal thinking.

The conclusion was that much of the science education being offered to the majority of students required formal and abstract thinking, beyond the ability of the majority of students to make sense of it. The problem-solving approach suited the gifted student since in the Nuffield style science they were asked to 'discover for themselves' and this heuristic approach favours the gifted student whose higher metacognitive levels enable them to be capable of independent and self-generated styles of learning. Indeed this probabilistic approach is highly desirable to prevent them developing the hierarchical 'box-like', right-answer thinking styles so conductive to high academic attainment upon simple question and answer style tests.

The dissatisfaction with the limited science education of the 1970–80s led to the action-research approach of Secondary Science Curriculum Review (SSCR) of the 1980s. Development of the research that came from the classrooms involved in the research made teachers strive to make the science more appropriate for differing abilities and groups of students and heralded the concept of differentiation in science education for all students.

From the work of the SSCR many good things were identified which would benefit all students and its conclusions influenced government opinion so much that *Science 5–16: A statement of policy* (DES 1985) was published which signalled a change in emphasis in science education. It was never to be developed fully because the next development was the institution of the National Curriculum in 1989 and science as a core subject. This original curriculum with its 17 attainment targets embodied many of the developments from the SSCR and the nationwide science education research but it was too cumbersome in its design. The subsequent revision of the science National Curriculum in 1991 led to a slimmer structure but one with more content condensed into fewer attainment targets.

It could be argued paradoxically that this slimming process has resulted in the removal of any heurism in present day science education and since this does appear to be the most effective way of teaching the gifted student it is to be regretted. It is, however, still a current debate since the approach to science education has been affected by the perceived view that there has to be a heavy reliance on the study of all the content of the National Curriculum programmes of study in order for every student to be able to demonstrate good academic performance in the end of key stage tests. This is however more a development of teacher confidence that they have covered all aspects so all pupils have been given the opportunity to reach all levels. Sadly this quantity versus quality debate has led to a restrictive curriculum for the gifted student in science.

The lack of some science departments making a careful examination of the progression in the level descriptions and using that progression as an indicator of the expectations for differing abilities of pupils has driven a proportion of science education in English schools towards a more transmission style of teaching science, without clear consideration of the relevance of science to everyday life and society. Also it has led to a lack of high level thinking, which had been a characteristic of the Nuffield heuristic approach.

Shayer and Adey picked up on the area of emphasising thinking skills in their development of Cognitive Acceleration through Science Education (CASE) (Shayer and Adey 1994) in order to encourage the thinking of students. Much academic research indicates it works well in developing confidence in thinking skills for the average student and for the gifted pupil it helps to consolidate the thinking processes needed to deal with abstract concepts. However there has been some criticism that the examples are not sufficiently challenging when used in mixed ability groups and the function of the gifted student is to act as peer teacher. The gain in this circumstance could well be only in the development of social skills. However examination of the structure of CASE allows teachers to develop an approach to planning science for all abilities using the concept of cognitive conflict in a student's thinking.

Cognitive conflict means presenting the student with an observation or problem that cannot be readily explained or solved using his or her own present ideas. This does not allow the student to make a clear predictive reason for the event or observation but causes the student to explain using their reasoning ability.

Success in the cognitive conflict activity depends upon how well the student relates to experience and inductive thinking, or is capable of inferential thinking using all aspects of the evidence. Many gifted pupils are more than capable of this style of thinking but more importantly cognitive conflict can lead to the exposure and challenging of **alternative concepts** or **misconceptions** in the student's mind.

Central to Shayer and Adey's CASE approach is Vygotsky's (1962) concept of the **Zone of Proximal Development**. This is defined as the difference between what the student can do on their own and what they can do if supported by more able peers or adults through carefully designed activities.

The criticism has been made that in most cognitive conflict situations the gifted student often takes the role of the teacher by questioning the ideas of the others. Plus the results of recent research on cooperative work that this situation may not serve to afford the gifted pupil any cognitive challenge, it could be argued that in the CASE lesson, there is more of an affective rather than cognitive challenge and, though this is not to be discouraged, a teacher needs to be aware of this and plan to offer some other cognitive challenge to the gifted pupil at other times. The following example uses the idea of cognitive challenge but uses conflicting concepts to afford that.

Example of using cognitive processes to solve a problem

The burning candle

Work in small groups of three to discuss for 10 minutes the following problem.

An ordinary long wax candle of 2 cm diameter and 15 cm length is weighted at the flat base end with modelling clay to enable it to float upright in a deep tank of cold water. The wick is exposed and is lit and allowed to burn in a room with no major draughts from windows or doors.

It burns over an extended period of time – three hours. What will happen to the candle over that period of time? Explain your deductions using appropriate science ideas.

Come back together as a larger group and discuss your collective views and examine, test and challenge each other's science ideas to reach a collective view. When you have reached a collective view try out the problem and see if you were right. Explain any result that is counter to what you thought would happen.

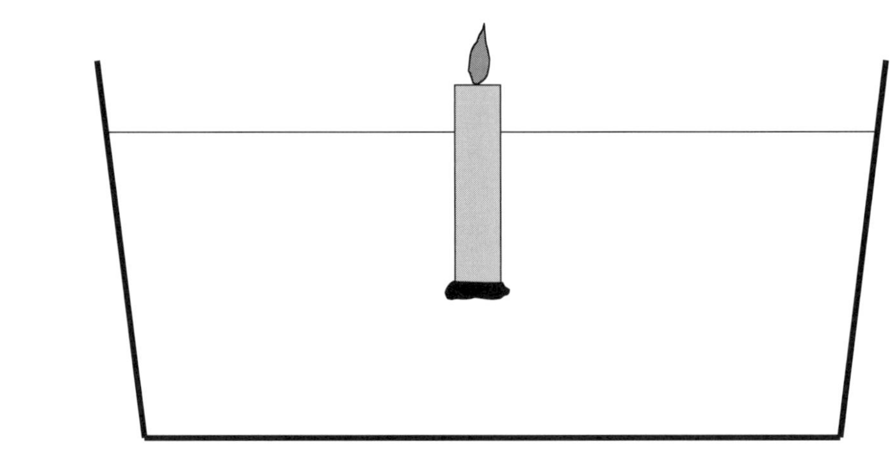

The candle problem is, on the surface, a relatively simple problem closely related to those Christmas candles that burn floating on water. However, the difference is the addition of the stabilising mass of modelling clay which will not change its mass as the candle will slowly loose mass with the combustion of the wax by the flame. This will adjust the problem and will cause the student to think of floating and sinking and Archimedes' conclusions on floating and sinking objects. Others will consider the problem as more about combustion and the melting of wax down the candle sides to form a stable floating 'outrigger' to keep the candle upright. The solution is, in fact, more connected with the conduction of heat and the cooling effect of the cold water on the candle wax surrounding the flame.

Thinking lessons in science can pick up on the scaffolding structure of CASE to develop a lesson plan for all abilities and to enable teachers to design for the gifted pupil. In CASE there are five distinct and important parts to the lesson:

- **Concrete preparation** – This is the introduction and sets the scene of the activity. In this stage the teacher sets out the objectives and makes explicit the links to previous work done by the student. In this stage vocabulary developed previously is established with meanings, previous processes are called to mind and contexts used to develop the ideas are used as starting points. This stage of the lesson is teacher directed.

- **Cognitive conflict** – This is the stage where the student's ideas are challenged by activities. In this stage the student's alternative concepts or misconceptions are revealed. These are challenges to the student's thinking. This stage will require discussion around an activity and can work well if groups are composed very carefully so that the more able can promote discussion with the least able in secure surroundings. This section will flow naturally into the next stage.
- **Construction** – It is in this stage that the teacher sets out activities that help the student to reconstruct their ideas and hopefully move towards an appropriate construct for thinking through the problem. This may not always be a fully accurate idea as set against present science thinking, but is a step along the route and closer to the accepted paradigm. These stages will be different for different groups of student.
- **Metacognition** – This is the discussion stage where the students discuss the ideas and use the language of the subject to construct concepts in their own mind. This again will work well if groups are constructed very carefully to allow good constructive, challenging discussion to take place in secure surroundings.
- **Bridging** – This is a teacher directed discussion in which the strategy or concept is elucidated, language and convention established. It is also during this that bridging to other situations where this thinking strategy can be used is discussed. In this stage the subject knowledge and the cognitive strategies are established.

The teacher's skill is to control the cognitive conflict of the activities by supporting the student in discussions and activities helping them to cross their Zone of Proximal Development and then to lead or direct the student in the construction of meaning or scaffolding by use of appropriate thinking processes. This is the act of bridging where the thinking skills learnt are taken into the mainstream curriculum. The teacher and student examine the thinking used and think where else that style of thinking can be used effectively. Effective teachers accomplish this act of bridging by getting the students to:

- use explanations, demonstrations, stories and analogies to develop models to explain concepts. The gifted will engage in these activities for themselves but may need some guidance and direction to prevent them going off onto tangents.
- develop language skills to enable them to explain and define ideas using verbal concepts to describe and define events. The gifted student will use precise science language and conventions, so here differing genres for writing can be used to develop their skills.
- learn to listen carefully, to value and question other people's explanations and to reason out an explanation that relies on evidence to support the explanation. Gifted students can manage this for themselves using peer- and self-criticism.
- Gain the confidence to learn and accept other people's help to help them to learn. In mixed ability groups the gifted student is often the peer facilitator and teacher so to develop this for the gifted student they need others of comparable or higher ability working with them. This can be accomplished by using sixth form mentors or vertical groups of students.

- support the learning of the least able student in the class. In mixed ability classes care needs to be taken that this does not outweigh the number of occasions the gifted student is cognitively challenged on his or her own level, particularly if there are only one or two gifted students in the group.

The success of this approach lies in three main things:

- First, the cognitive challenge or support of the language and the opportunity to reflect by discussion on the ideas relating variables, concepts and models. This is the concrete examination of the concepts.
- Second, the thinking strategies and the student sharing those ideas by practical example. This is the metacognition aspect.
- Third, the teacher's challenging the student to think where else in their thinking the strategy can be used. The so-called bridging activity can be achieved by:
  - examining the context and constructing the thinking strategy and matching the thinking to other contexts where the approach would work.
  - identifying the reasoning pattern by working with the class to identify the steps in the logic of solving the problem. In this the strategies are the main concentration for the learning.
  - collaborative learning where students discuss in groups the procedures they have undergone to achieve the solution. This examines the thinking strategy and allows the student to develop his or her own models for thinking.

Developing thinking for the gifted student in science

McGuinness (1999) in the Northern Ireland's Activating Children's Thinking (ACT's) project on thinking showed from their research there is a need for a general framework for teaching thinking. Using that evidence it is possible to argue the following progression in developing thinking for the gifted science students:

- Thinking skills should be made explicit in the science curriculum and for the gifted these should be the higher order thinking skills of analysis, synthesis and evaluation. Hence they should be engaged in thought experiments around problems in which the solution is not immediately obvious. For example those found in *The Science of Superheroes* (Gresh and Weinberg 2002) where the discussion surrounds the science and the possibility of the existence of superheroes or *How to Dunk a Doughnut* (Fisher 2002) in which the science of everyday things is discussed or Fullick and Ratcliffe (1996), which presents some of the ethical arguments in science.
- Students coached to develop the application of higher order thinking skills in novel ways allowing them to develop fluidity between creative and critical thinking. Examination of the events and the strange accidents that lead to great developments in science such as in *Serendipity: Accidental discoveries in science* (Roberts 1989), *The Pinball Effect* (Burke 1996), PRI-Pupil Research Initiative (Collins 2001) or Ideas and Evidence (Folens 2002).
- Thinking should be taught in a metacognitive frame to allow bridging (uses of similar thinking in different contexts) to take place and the student to concentrate on this aspect to identify advanced learning skills. Advanced mapping and thinking frameworks should be used to enable the student to

learn different strategies for thinking, using examples from Ewy (2003) and Centre for Management Creativity (2002).

- Collaborative learning using both ICT and face-to-face approaches should be used in a balanced way to develop independent and self-generated learning. Some of the software developed for the Open University S103 course can be very helpful here since it will allow the student to engage in independent learning. For example *Galapagos: Adaptation and evolution on islands* and *A Geological Field Trip* (Open University 1999) and Science Web Readers (Nelson Thornes 2000) which allow the student to learn about concepts and test ideas for themselves.
- Thinking should be developed in a science framework embodying 'thinking classrooms' and 'thinking schools' through the whole curriculum and not through special skills lessons.

McGuinness *et al.* (1996) showed that thinking should not be seen as a bolt-on activity but one firmly embedded in a subject and that thinking needs real contexts, students need a role through which their thinking processes can channel, an audience at which their work is directed and will direct styles and form of communication structures required. McGuinness *et al.* identify the following types of cognitive activity to develop effective thinking skills:

- planning, testing solutions, relating causes and effects and designing fair tests, making predictions and hypothesising;
- generating new ideas by brainstorming, problem solving, thinking of alternative solutions;
- sequencing, ordering, sorting, classifying and grouping information;
- analysing – part and whole relationships – by comparing and contrasting;
- making decisions and weighing up pros and cons, distinguishing fact from opinion, determining bias and checking the reliability of the evidence;
- drawing conclusions, giving reasons from the evidence available.

Summary

1. Meeting the explicitness of thinking skills in science: the National Curriculum lists five thinking skills that act as a complement to the key skills and these are the same skills that need to be developed for the gifted and the average student but in different contexts. These skills are:
   - **Information-processing skills** – students to collect, sort, classify, sequence, compare and contrast, and analyse information, evidence and data to identify the patterns and relationships that exist in that material.
   - **Reasoning skills** – students to use precise language to define concepts, give reasons for their opinions and decisions and explain their ideas.
   - **Enquiry skills** – students to develop the ability to ask questions that are relevant to an event, problem or phenomenon, to pose questions for researching, exploring, to produce predictions, anticipate consequences with regard to errors, inaccuracies and reliability.

- **Creative thinking skills** – students to develop the ability to generate ideas using previous known ideas and facts and use their imagination in order to search for alternative solutions.
- **Evaluation skills** – students to validate and evaluate information and conclusions by developing criteria for making valued judgements on their own and others' thinking.

The posing of cognitive challenges by CASE style activities can approach this, or the posing of demanding **problem-solving** activities to enable them to exercise creativity by the use of **thought experiments**. This should be accompanied by **metacognition** focusing on the discussion of thinking strategies and getting the student to identify where they can see bridging in their own learning.

2. Collaborative learning needs some care with gifted students since tasks set for most teaching groups, particularly mixed ability, will not necessarily challenge the gifted without active differentiation and some research indicates that in many cases the only challenge for them in collaborative learning is in the affective realm. Some work has been done in using **grouping by abilities** for some activities and has been found to be especially useful since objectives can be set relating to their level of learning. This will allow effective **content extension** of the science curriculum for the student.
3. Clear identification of an **abstract or unfamiliar context** with a focused **role** for the gifted learner and an **audience** and **genre** to write for. This allows for challenge for the gifted student by lateral extension that can be called **context enrichment** of the science curriculum for the student.
4. **ICT** is a good **facilitator** of **independent learning** and can be used very effectively with gifted students if the software is demanding and promotes thinking by setting up problems.
5. Some gifted students will benefit from professional **coaching** with older students such as sixth formers, mentors or links with professionals in industry or universities.
6. Use of curriculum enrichment by the staging of masterclasses to allow gifted students the opportunity to explore a complete problem in a realistic fashion. Extending the learning by attendance at appropriate lectures such as the Royal Institution lectures or by linking with PhD students in research activities.

CHAPTER 5

Assessing Understanding to Develop Thinking Skills

The teacher's role is to help the student move through the Zone of Proximal Development by supporting the student with intervention, facilitating or setting up teaching activities that allow the student the independence to work alone on what they can do and also on those areas where they would need help. To do this effectively requires a balance of different types of assessment:

- **Diagnostic assessment** seeks to find out what the weaknesses are in the student's science learning, to determine why it is weak, share that information with the student in the form of learning targets and then, in partnership with the student, to set about rectifying and developing the learning as well as possible. As was shown by Sternberg (1994) a gifted pupil will not be globally gifted but selectively gifted so diagnostic assessment by the use of concept cartooning, prediction–observation–explanation and concept mapping is just as important for the gifted science student as for the least able. However the gifted have the capacity to monitor their own progress towards targets using logbooks of progress and self-criticism, interviews or peer-discussion on their learning.
- **Formative assessment** informs both teacher and student how well the learning process is progressing against specific science learning objectives and for this to be effective those learning objectives need to be shared and understood. To enable differentiation to be understood by the student the objectives need to be tiered and linked and revisited at the end of a lesson to enable the gifted student to determine how well they have progressed towards those objectives. A science teacher's day-to-day assessment of the student's written, drawn and spoken work will be against these objectives and, if the teacher and student have a constant record of the objectives, they have a means of checking learning through a varied means of assessment.
- **Summative assessment** indicates the 'milestones' reached in terms of key principles or ideas relating to the science topic covered in that period of time. They are measured against the full set of learning objectives linked to learning outcomes which are assessed and quoted as the mark of attainment and when measured against the starting point marks the progression in learning. This should test understanding as well as knowledge but it is often limited to relatively low level thinking tasks related to question and answer style

assessment. However the use of concept mapping, flow diagrams, flash cards and concept cartoons can vary the assessment diet and provide more information about understanding.

The primary difficulty in designing forms of assessment, especially summative, is that of actually describing what understanding means in a science topic, for example knowledge, concept depth, methodology, or culture. Most forms of assessment assess knowledge alone and use the lower order thinking skills while the higher order skills, that will show deeper levels of understanding, are frequently not used effectively.

In the main, gifted pupils will show high attainment on the lower order thinking skills and so in most question and answer tests that assess knowledge they obtain high marks. The gifted pupils require activities that test the higher orders of thinking such as analysis, synthesis and evaluation. To clarify the areas of understanding there are six possible targets in relation to our learning in science:

- **Units of knowledge in science** – learning specific facts in all areas of science. These are regulated by rules of logic meaning. Students do not have to understand all the ideas but can be successful by linking ideas by association or description using experiential explanations or analogies. This leads to the use of misconceptions in the student's knowledge. Though this area is frequently tested by question and answer techniques more useful information can be obtained by the use of concept cartoons, concept mapping and problem solving.
- **Concepts in science** – assigning meaning to things and phenomena using specific science language, models and reasoning skills to reduce arguments or reconstruct ideas to specific meanings embodied in phrases, words, symbols or mathematical models. This is generally assessed by comprehension activities involving the reconstruction of models, diagrams or remodelling text, or introspective debate upon a concept cartoon followed by group challenge.
- **Communication of science** – the understanding of a process of communication, for example writing, talk, prose, drama, poem, dance or illustration. Question and answer procedures demonstrate the ability to communicate the immediate factors and explain them but often the underlying meanings that require the use of conventions or symbolism are not developed, as in chemistry or physics equations. This is generally assessed by compositional writing, posters or presentations in different genres requiring interpretation of science conventions into daily language or the reverse, daily experiences into science conventions.
- **Situations in science** – information presented instantaneously and not specifically sequentially, in which students select information to make sense. This is frequently reliant upon points of view and beliefs that lead to predictive thinking such as in a science investigation or exploration. It is generally assessed by focus upon enquiry skills, that is manipulation of data or evidence collected from an experiment, or sifting evidence using tools such as developing reductive arguments by the use of zones of relevance (see Chapter 6) using argument mapping (see Chapter 6) to balance evidence against rebuttals or the evaluation of evidence in a case study.
- **Organisation of discipline** – a subjective internal decision-making process in which we make conscious efforts to learn and organise science knowledge in our own personal style. This makes use of metacognition and the way the student thinks about things so it is frequently assessed by lists of key words

with definitions, flow charts of concepts, herring-bone diagrams, mind or concept mapping, or brainstorming.

- **Personal reaction to science** – a subjective process of explaining why a person reacts as they do leading the student into predictive thinking to confirm their beliefs and viewpoints. This is generally assessed by SWOT (Strengths, Weaknesses, Opportunities and Threats) analysis of case studies and contrast grids indicating strengths and weaknesses or similarities and differences and emphasis and bullet pointing.

(Adapted from Gunstone and White 1992)

Gunstone and White argue that understanding is a process of linking personal knowledge of an event or phenomenon to the observations made and then making predictions about future events or phenomena. This leads to the essential idea that the individual constructs meaning for themselves and it develops as the individual adds more elements to his or her existing knowledge pattern.

Construction takes place as a result of cognitive conflict followed by acts of reflection, through incidental learning and through the action of teaching. Hence the teacher must make use of a wide range of assessment techniques for the full range of abilities but more so to gain an objective view of the gifted science student. This is particularly true when the teacher has both academically able and cognitively able students, since the academically able will score high in assessments but the cognitively able student may only present their ability when the task interests them; up to that point they will do comfortably well enough to secure a position of security. This need for a range of assessment tools makes evaluation of a student's understanding too complex to be reduced to a simple numerical score.

The construction of meaning in any subject by directed and focused thinking relies heavily upon the student reflecting upon given ideas and evidence and looking for patterns to explain. In this mode of learning, the student can learn routines and be successful within given ranges of learning, but the mark of the gifted student is the ability to seek their own patterns in diffuse but connected data, form a conclusion and evaluate the success of that action.

This self-generated process of logic means the gifted student develops and evaluates their own reasoning patterns and uses thinking strategies to discuss and think about the problem.

Implicit in this approach for many students is the need to have confident verbal skills when dealing with text on the page and in conversation. Weakness in the verbal skills, particularly when dealing with the logic in written text, can lead to a lack of risk taking in the student's learning skills and produce low motivation or frustration in the student.

This verbal difficulty is not uncommon in science and is often the case with gifted science students who can see the way to solve a problem-style question when dealing with it in spoken language, but is confronted by the written language. Science uses a integral mixture of word symbols, numerical manipulation and abstract symbols to build models. However, since the text language is a major part of the cognitive challenge in science, with its specificity of language, this needs careful management in the science classroom to develop some of the gifted students whose flairs in reasoning lie in mathematical and abstract modelling. This consideration of the interaction of verbal skills and other learning skills encourages the student to become conscious of their own thinking processes and makes use of metacognition.

The difficulty for teachers dealing with gifted students who display weaknesses in verbal skills is attempting to adequately assess the student and offer a diet appropriate to support this gifted science student. Central to the problem is the environment the student has come through to reach secondary school, since this will affect the development of their metacognition and perception of the subject, which in turn affects their cognition skills and intellect in science.

Gifted students who display high levels of metacognition will often make decisions about the lack of importance of the work to them, can shun school work and learn for themselves by engaging in project work in their own time. They can become expert in areas of science not generally covered in any depth in school science, for example astrophysics, electronics, geophysics, meteorology, etc. Boys often fit this style since some boys learn in secret and play in public and so they often resent open praise for successful performance. Hence they can hide their gifts under a screen of doing just enough in school to succeed but outside school, using the Internet and libraries, they develop a high level of intellect in a subject. This can often come to light in unexpected situations such as discussions with parents or pupil interviews with mentors or in masterclass situations.

Students from culturally diverse backgrounds may meet blocks in their thinking because they think in their 'mother-tongue' and do not see the nuances of the debate because of the fine detail of the science language. Experiments by English As A Second Language (EAL) teachers can help as key information is translated into the student's 'mother-tongue', the student is expected to think about the topic in their own language and then translate the answer into English. This means the student is using their own language to learn in but English as the language of communication.

Students from culturally poor backgrounds often have not had the full range of experiences to develop their linguistic skills or reasoning skills and yet all these individuals can display characteristics that develop late in their lives and, if uncovered, would deem them to be gifted in school. These gifted students need careful support with thinking and communication frameworks that support communication but allow free thinking. It is often more important to get the student's ideas and concepts down in notes through the use of storyboarding and bullet points or by cartooning and then as a group exercise model the writing to determine style and effective communication.

Science has had its fair share of those individuals who either found school uninspiring or school found them deficient. Famous examples of students who showed science skills seemingly without school support are: Isaac Newton, seen as not very bright when he was a schoolboy; Albert Einstein, who shunned academic work offered to him; and Richard Feynman, who found schoolwork uninspiring.

To be effective learners gifted students need to display high levels of metacognition to promote motivation to be independent and responsible thinkers and learners. To be metacognitive thinkers all students need time to reflect upon how to and how they have solved the problem and what they found difficult. In Vygotsky's (1978) concept of the Zone of Proximal Development (the difference between the actual level of problem solving displayed by the student and the potential level that can be developed by careful teaching), the process of learning is a dual action between the interpersonal action of discussion and the process of cognition – thinking. For example an individual Year 7 student can solve simple cause and effect problems, such as solution A mixed with solution B will produce substances C and D, independently. They can solve some simple word equations with guidance from the teacher but cannot solve balanced symbol chemical equations no matter how much help they are given. It would be fair to say word chemical equations are within the student's Zone of Proximal Development, and this is the most effective level to offer instruction. It would be of little use presenting the student with observational cause and effect problems they can already solve, or to present balanced symbol chemical equations problems that will only frustrate them. However the gifted student in a mixed ability class may be capable, with assistance from the teacher, of solving a balanced chemical equation.

In an assessment situation the teacher is attempting to determine the range of the Zone of Proximal Development so a student's non-attempt or failure to secure a correct answer may indicate this range for that student. Often the gifted student will get the highest marks and the teacher may miss the significance of this, that is the gifted student may be insufficiently challenged by the task hence they should continue to challenge the student with harder problems until the range of the Zone of Proximal Development has been ascertained.

Also in an assessment situation the student has to engage in intrapersonal reflection and debate and if the answer is a straightforward statement of fact or application of fact, if they know the answer, the gifted student will find the task easy. It is in an analysis, synthesis and evaluation situation that the reflection and personal debate becomes important. It is for that reason the range of assessment for the gifted will need to be extensive.

The teacher's role in supporting a student in the Zone of Proximal Development is to assess for starting points and then provide the student with scaffolds or schemata – patterns of reasoning that help formal thought. These patterns of thought are not unique to that problem but can be applied to other similar problems so teachers need to examine, with the student, those schemata and help the student see where they can apply those ideas in other areas of science.

The gifted student will frequently take note of these patterns of thought and learn to transfer their skills well, but some will need help to learn to examine these thinking strategies and learn to transfer them. This is particularly true where the student has come through a very restrictive science course designed to develop knowledge rather than thinking scientifically.

These gifted students frequently show high performance in tests but are insecure in situations where the argument is a probabilistic one. They frequently ask if this is the 'right' answer and can become frustrated if there is no absolute answer. This can affect their perception of the subject and they would need contact with real scientists to reassure them.

The key to this is effective formative assessment and gifted students take close notice of the comments more than the marks in order to improve their learning. They are also more involved in self-assessment and evaluation of their own learning. This is a mark of high metacognitive development and gifted students often show levels two or more years ahead of their peers. This observation matches well with the findings of the Assessment Reform Group (1999) where it indicated that effective learning for all pupils takes place when:

- effective feedback to students is provided in relation to the learning objectives;
- students are involved in their own learning by taking decisions about their learning;
- diagnostic assessment is undertaken, it is used to adjust the teaching and the progress is recorded through the use of formative assessment;

- the influence of assessment on self-esteem and motivation is recognised by the teacher and success is celebrated;
- students have the opportunity to assess and evaluate their own learning and know how they can improve their learning.

It therefore becomes important to involve the gifted science student in their own assessment of their learning. This can be achieved by the use of personal logbooks in which personal targets are stated and students comment on their progress towards these. Alongside those comments is a requirement for the student to comment on the way the science knowledge affects their thinking about the world. This is to develop in the student the concept of a culture of science rather than just the need to learn science to pass an examination.

A more personal approach to the assessment and development of metacognition to promote self-esteem can be achieved by the use of sixth formers or teachers as mentors to discuss the work and how it is progressing and how it affects the student. David Leat at Newcastle University calls this process debriefing since it provides a dialogue in which science can form connections with other areas of learning.

How to assess thinking

This chapter concludes with three examples of exercises that can be used to assess a student's ability to think. In each case the student is required to answer questions using the information supplied.

Examples of tasks to assess thinking – Adapted from Science Web 2 (Horsfall, O'Brien, Macdonald and Murphy 2002)

Puerperal fever

Puerperal fever has been known since Greek times. Hippocrates (died 357 BCE – Before Common Era) states that just after birth is a dangerous time for a woman because of fever that can result in death. He institutes the use of obstetric forceps to lower the need for hand contact.

18th Century, Britain: Some doctors realise puerperal fever can be carried from one patient to another.

1790, Dublin: Joseph Clark and Robert Collins lower the mortality of women in childbirth by maintaining clean conditions – washing bedding, burning sulphur to fumigate and isolating patients. This is not accepted as reasonable and they are attacked as being ridiculous. Old practices return and so does the disease.

1823, Vienna: In the German Hospital, housing the biggest maternity clinic in the world, students learn on a dummy and the mortality rate in the maternity clinic is 1–2%. Boer, the present Professor of Obstetrics, retires.

1823: Klein is appointed as Professor of Obstetrics at the German Hospital. Students now learn by examination of patients and autopsies.

1840s, Boston USA: Oliver Wendell Holmes finds puerperal fever disease among his women patients. He adopts Clark's practice and finds it working in reducing the number of mortalities.

1843: He publishes a paper but is ridiculed for his ideas.

1845: Mortality in the German Hospital increases to 7% in the ward with doctors and students but remains at 2% in the ward where midwives deliver the babies.

1846: Semmeiweis, an Hungarian nationalist, becomes the assistant to Klein and between January and May 1847 mortality is 12–13%.

1847, May: Semmeiweis makes all doctors wash their hands in a chlorinated wash. The mortality rate in the ward drops to 1–1.5%. Semmeiweis experiments by introducing autopsy material into the vagina of live rabbits. They soon die from fever.

1850: Semmeiweis is dismissed. He returns to Hungary.

1855: He is appointed to the Chair of Obstetrics in Pest. Hospitals in his care adopt his methods and the mortality rate drops.

1861: Semmeiweis publishes a book on the prevention of childbed fever. The ideas are accepted in Hungary. Doctors in Vienna continue to attack him in medical papers.

1865: He suffers a mental breakdown and is admitted to a mental hospital where he dies. The cause of his death is not clear. Beating by attendants is suspected.

1869, London: Joseph Lister uses carbonic acid during his operations and the mortality rate decreases. Carbonic acid is recognised as a useful antiseptic, that is a substance that kills or stops the growth of bacteria.

1886, Germany: Professor Ernst von Bergmann and Professor Gustav Neuber create aseptic conditions (i.e. conditions free from micro-organisms) in a room used for operations. It is washed with carbonic acid, all the instruments are boiled and the surgeons wear sterilised gowns, masks, caps and rubber aprons. The mortality rate decreases even more.

Questions

1. Look at the evidence in the text and write a paragraph discussing what it tells you about puerperal fever and the way it is spread.
2. Use the above information to write a short article for the local newspaper giving the evidence for a bacterial or viral cause and possible solutions to lessen the spread of the disease.
3. Plot a graph of the changes in mortality in the maternity clinic in the German Hospital, Vienna, 1823–1847 and justify the conclusions Semmeiweis came to using the changes in data.

How much of limestone is calcium carbonate?

All limestone samples have at least 50 per cent calcium carbonate in them. Different limestones will have differing amounts of calcium carbonate in them that tell geologists something about the conditions the rock was made in. The differing proportions of calcium carbonate also affect the rock and its use for building. The other factor that will affect its use for building will be the size and number of fossil shells in the rock. Building technologists examine rock samples to determine which are best for building.

An example of poor choice can be seen in London. St Paul's Cathedral was built in the 17th century of very fine limestone and has not needed a great deal of re-building or refurbishment. However the Palace of Westminster built in the 19th century was made from poorer quality limestone with many fossils in it and the rocks were laid in the wrong way. The result is up to 70 per cent is refurbished stone replacing the worn stone.

It is possible to use simple chemical reactions to find out which limestone sample contains the most calcium carbonate. When an acid reacts with crushed calcium carbonate, the gas carbon dioxide is produced. The more calcium carbonate is present, the more acid will be needed to react with it and the more carbon dioxide gas will be produced. Here are some results from an analysis of three types of limestone. Each rock sample is weighed dry at the start of the reaction and is dried again before weighing after the reaction.

Type of limestone used	Mass of limestone used (g)	Time taken for the completion of the reaction
Brown limestone	3	1 minute 15 seconds
White limestone	3	1 minute 40 seconds
Soft limestone	3	1 minute 50 seconds

Type of limestone	Mass of limestone used (g)	Volume of carbon dioxide produced (cm^3)
Brown limestone	3	15
White limestone	3	20
Soft limestone	3	24

Type of limestone	Mass of limestone used (g)	Mass of limestone left after reaction (g)
Brown limestone	3	1.4
White limestone	3	0.8
Soft limestone	3	0.4

1. Explain why you think the samples of limestone should be crushed.
2. Explain why any sample of limestone is dried after the reaction before being weighed again.
3. Explain why it is important for each sample of limestone to be the same mass.
4. Explain why it would be right to use different strengths of acid in one of the tests.
5. In the last test the same strength and amount of acid was used so why is some limestone left and in differing amounts from the different limestone types?
6. If low levels of calcium carbonate is one feature the technologist is looking for in a rock suitable for building, which of the above samples would be suitable and why?
7. Evaluate the evidence from the experiments and write a report for a building company intending to use limestone for the facing on a building in a city where there is heavy traffic and high rainfall.

Controversy in light

Light travels at the amazing speed of 300,000 km/s. The nearest star to the Earth (apart from the Sun) is so far away that the light from it takes four years to get to us. There are some stars that are so far away that light has taken several billion years to get to us. These stars may have blown up thousands of years ago but we cannot know until we see the explosion in the night sky. When we look at the night sky we are really looking back in time towards the beginning of the universe. If we see an explosion it must have happened a long time ago because the light takes a long time to travel to us. This means we can never know what the universe is like now!

When light travels through space and travels close to a star it is bent, so making it necessary to calculate the actual position of the star compared to the apparent position. The universe is expanding and so as the light travels to the Earth through the universe it is affected by the Doppler Effect, where the waves are bunched closer together, as an object comes closer to us, or stretched out as the object moves away from us. These shifts can be observed when the light is split up and the red and blue ends examined.

Nothing can travel faster than light. Some scientists have predicted that there are some particles called tachyons, which do travel faster than light. If ever they find one then they will have to change many of their theories about how the universe works. In the equation $E = mc^2$ Einstein postulated that energy and mass are interchangeable by this formula. In 1930 Subrahmanyan Chandrasekhar (known as Chandra), an Indian astrophysicist, took the ideas further and argued that when stars collapsed, because of the formula gravity is ratcheted up and this can result in a 'Black Hole'. In England he received little support for the idea so he moved to the USA and in 1983 received the Nobel Prize for his work.

1. Calculate how many kilometres between the nearest star and us.
2. Explain what the implications of these ideas are for light coming from the Earth to another planet that could be orbiting another distant star in the universe.
3. Explain why you think the discovery of a particle travelling faster than light would be A. Exciting and B. Controversial for science.
4. It is sometimes said that light and time are linked. What does this mean to you?

CHAPTER 6

Implications for Teaching – Thinking

Developing higher level thinking processes in any student is dependent upon the social processes of learning, the use of the interpersonal and intrapersonal intelligences identified by Gardner. The development of activities in science for the gifted can make use of these intelligences by using differing types of context, levels of language, communication styles and mathematical skills as differentiating factors.

The above approach frequently makes the activity a cross-curricular one and the demand for cognitive skills to be used in multiple knowledge domains makes the task more difficult because of the inter-relationships between the differing contents. For example the effect of balanced forces can be examined by the study of different moving toys on Earth and the same toy in space, or by looking at the subject of reactivity from the viewpoint of the history of human development from the palaeolithic to the 20th century aluminium age. This can be followed by asking the student to prepare a report as a simple piece of reportage in a popular journal, or to prepare a learned paper for a textbook for their peers or for an audience of scientists.

The construction of meaning in science by directed thinking relies heavily upon the student reflecting upon ideas and evidence and looking for patterns to explain the events. This means the student has to develop reasoning patterns and use those reasoning skills to discuss and think about the problem and then to infer or predict events or outcomes. Gifted students are quick to pick up on the patterns so any questions should relate the interpretation and application of those patterns to explanations. These styles of activities typify the Vygotsky cognitive challenge approach and the construction of personal knowledge paradigms.

The common characteristic about what might be called personal knowledge is that individuals construct this knowledge and often hold those views alongside more conventional knowledge, hence the majority of people talk of the Sun moving across the sky even though they may understand very well the actual science. The implication of this is that the individual uses their learned knowledge as an intellectual tool to answer direct factual questions, but uses their own personal construct to solve problems and it is here that the misconceptions are revealed.

Learning a subject like science is like learning a language because the learning is not a hierarchy of fact but more a lateral network of concepts and facts, that involves the use of text, visual, mathematical, graphical, abstract and algebraic information. In each system the student must master and translate between different codes in which they can encode the information or concept.

Wittgenstein (1967) states that the code or language being used to encode the concept only becomes meaningful if it is used in an activity or action that is 'sense making'. The process of making sense is helped by conceptualising the activity within a role for an audience to help secure a system of conventions and genre for communication. Sizmur and Ashby (1997) describe the interaction of context, role and language in the diagram shown in Figure 6.1.

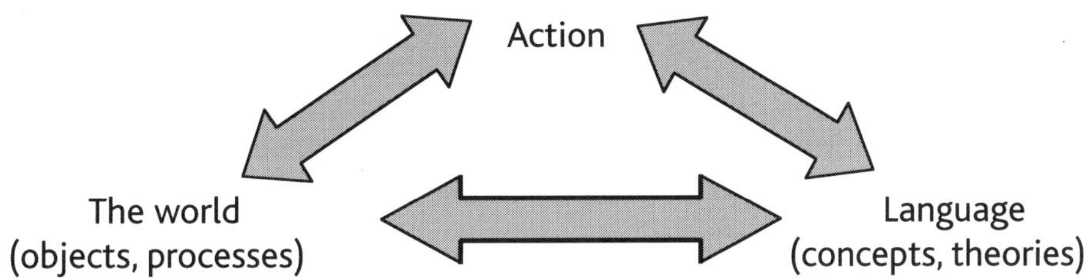

Figure 6.1 The interaction of context, role and language (Sizmur and Ashby 1997)

Theories and concepts in science become the focus of empirical research and this provides the evidence and allows predictions to be made and the gifted must be made to justify using science concepts and ideas. Sutton (1996) maintains that to help students learn, teachers should 'see as' the learner and understand where the thinking has led to alternative concepts and help to reconstruct ideas by thinking activities, involving language, that challenge the misconception.

There also has to be a balance between understanding the procedures and questioning the procedures of a subject to gain an understanding of why and how the process leads to an answer. This is the area of procedural understanding and should be linked to concepts to explain events or conceptual understanding in the use of carefully designed practical activities. Gifted students are more able in linking procedural understanding to conceptual understanding and this can be used to challenge the gifted science student in practical situations by asking them to justify the procedure.

Another approach is to challenge the students' thinking by asking them to explain how some everyday objects work, the choice of materials and the science behind those decisions. Rich areas for this type of activity are some executive toys, particularly those using fluids such as soothers, sand pictures or the balancing toys. Other useful toys for this sort of activity are flying or throwing toys, such as helicopters, paper and polymer gliders, ballistas or catapults, in which the aim is to redesign with a 'how accurate' or 'how far' objective for the toy. In this the student is encouraged to explain how their modification will work. Another source is to look at a simple tool and mentally take it apart with regard to how it works and the choice of material for its construction. The skills being developed are analysis of systems and relationships between concepts, explaining and justifying. Teachers should concentrate upon open questioning to encourage students to examine their explanations.

Implicit in the Vygotsky cognitive challenge approach is the need for confident verbal skills in dealing with both text and speech. Any weakness in a student's verbal skills can lead to a lack of risk taking in learning situations and produce low motivation or frustration for learning. Some students who come from backgrounds in which the stimulus and input has led to poorly developed linguistic skills but who display good science problem-solving skills can exhibit this. This can be helped by the use of other students acting as peer teachers in the use of text, but this requires carefully constructed learning objectives relating to paired reading use of thinking support techniques.

This active consideration of the interaction of verbal skills and learning skills encourages the students to become conscious of their own thinking processes – metacognition. For some gifted students this can be helped by the use of thinking maps and support materials. Generally writing frames can be considered thinking maps and aids but for the verbally gifted science student the over-prescription of a structure can be a deterrent to higher level thinking, so one needs to use other tools to develop the subject and use writing frames to model good writing skills.

To be effective metacognitive thinkers all students need time to reflect upon how they have solved the problem and what they found difficult. Teachers need to give all students the time to monitor their own learning and thinking and this is not just a function of mentoring but also a function of active learning. Gifted students need time to study thinking strategies and learn about reasoning structures in all abilities. It is in this way the student has learned to deal with the world around them; it is how they create meaning for themselves and express that meaning.

In his work Vygotsky also indicated the importance of developing scaffolds to assist the learner. This approach has been the basis of such work as Wray and Lewis's (1997) writing frameworks, Shayer and Adey's (1994) CASE (Cognitive Acceleration through Science Education) and concept mapping.

The brain does not work in a linear way; it works by making associations. Linear note taking is a routine learnt as a tool to organise information but only if the individual plays with the notes after to organise according to his or her personal thinking. The way the teacher or lecturer reveals the information relates more to the way they learnt it and their personal logic in organising it, but that might not be the same approach taken by the student. It is often better to teach students a range of visual tools that allow them the opportunity to organise the information as it is revealed. This will mean decisions being taken and the learner interacting with the information at the point of learning. They must not stay as visual diagrams but must have written contexts as well. This allows the pupil the opportunity to model genres for communication so completing the cycle text to spoken word and visuals to remodelled text. Novak and Gowin (1984) identify concept maps as diagrams that represent the meaningful relationships between concepts. They rest upon the development of propositions – two or more concept labels linked by words into a semantic unit. For example the linear sequence:

- Force is a push or pull.
- Force = mass × acceleration.
- Force is measured in Newton.

would become:

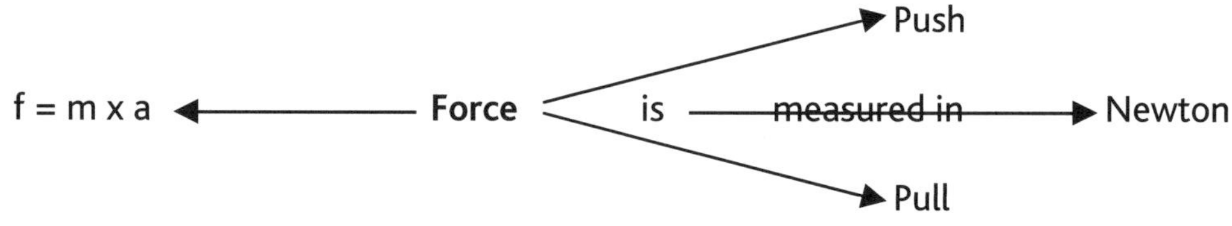

The arrows indicate the direction of the relationship in the semantic. They make clear the key ideas and language needed to understand the topic. They also allow the individual to organise ideas in their own way to help build their own mental models. For the gifted these tools help focus the thinking when working in higher level thinking levels and identify connections between ideas in science.

Thinking tools

There are a variety of tools that can be used to develop higher level thinking processes. Some are explained here.

Concept cycles

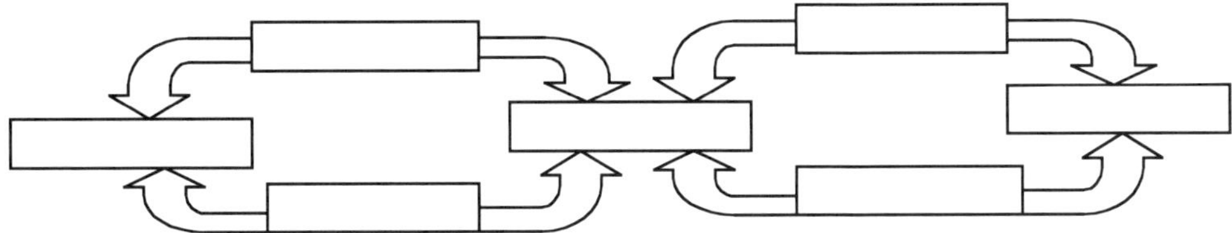

Figure 6.2 A concept cycle

A concept cycle (Figure 6.2) is a concept map used in science to show how events interact to produce a cycle of results. They are used frequently for the drawing of the water cycle, life cycles, the rock cycle or any cyclic process.

Network trees

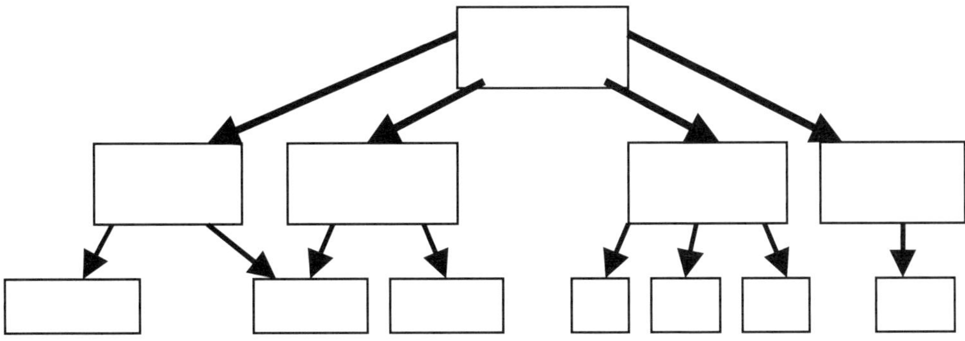

Figure 6.3 A network tree

A network tree (Figure 6.3) is a type of concept map that illustrates the hierarchy of subordinate relationships between concepts and shows the line of progression of ideas. Also it can be used to show causal relationships. Often in science it is used to show a progression of ideas, for example particle to atom to ion to molecule to sub-atomic particles, or for any classification process such as those for animals, plants or rocks. Other uses include for hierarchical relationships such as food chains, manufacturing processes or energy transforms.

Events chains

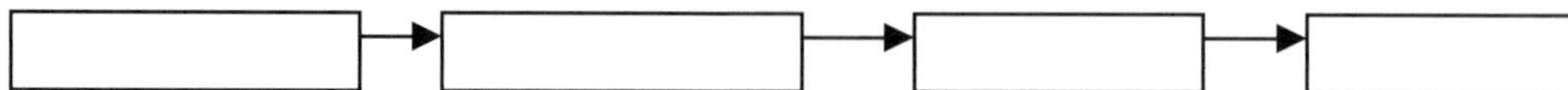

Figure 6.4 An events chain

Events chains (Figure 6.4) are concept maps that describe the stages of a process and they allow the pupil the opportunity to develop a linear relationship or sequence of events. This can be used as a flow chart to show a procedure in a technique, development of a formula or equation or a process such as the formation of soil from the weathering of rocks.

Consequence maps

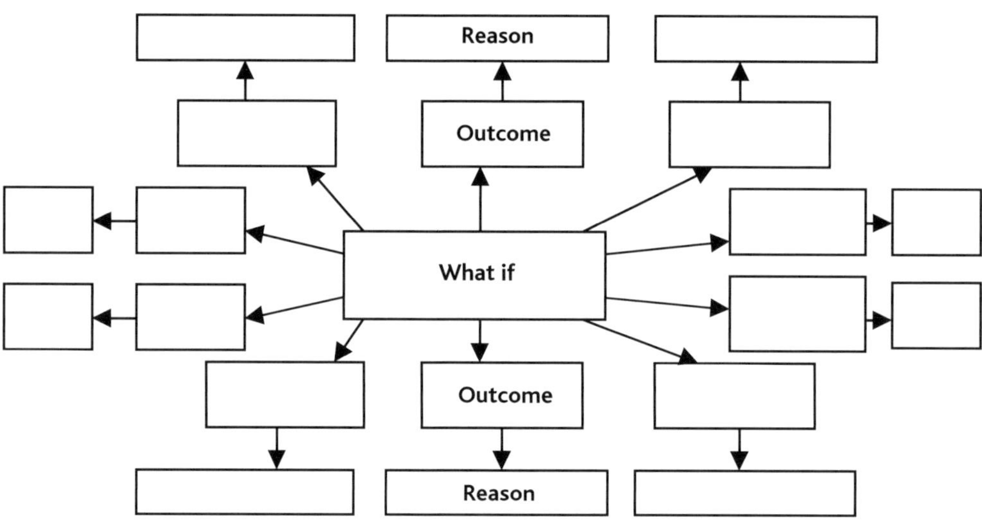

Figure 6.5 A consequence map

A consequence map (Figure 6.5) is a way of examining the multitude of consequences from an action or a proposed action. The student responds by identifying the outcomes to an action followed by the reasons for that outcome. These outcomes can be evaluated to ascertain the most probable outcome. These thinking tools are useful for all abilities but the gifted student responds more favourably than the average or less able student because they are capable of speculating upon and evaluating evidence. Consequence maps ask the student to make critical judgements, for example if the proposition was 'What would happen if gravity on Earth was reduced?'.

Vee heuristic diagram

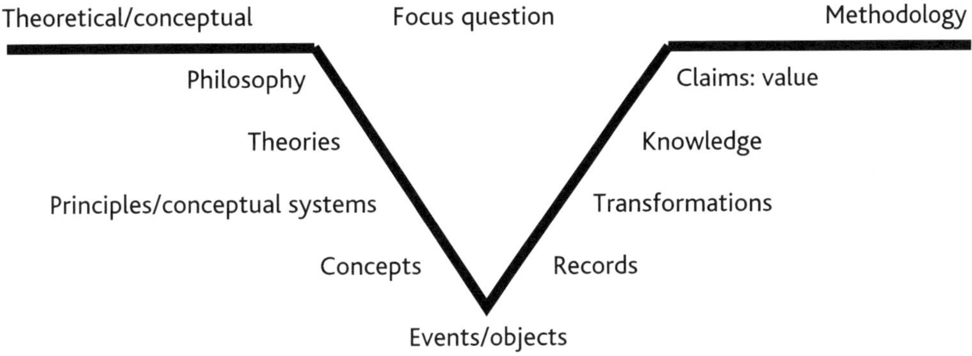

Figure 6.6 Vee heuristic diagram

A vee heuristic diagram (Figure 6.6) was developed to show the links between concepts and methodology and how they interact. It is a useful technique for analysis of documents, practical sessions and lectures.

Herring-bone diagrams

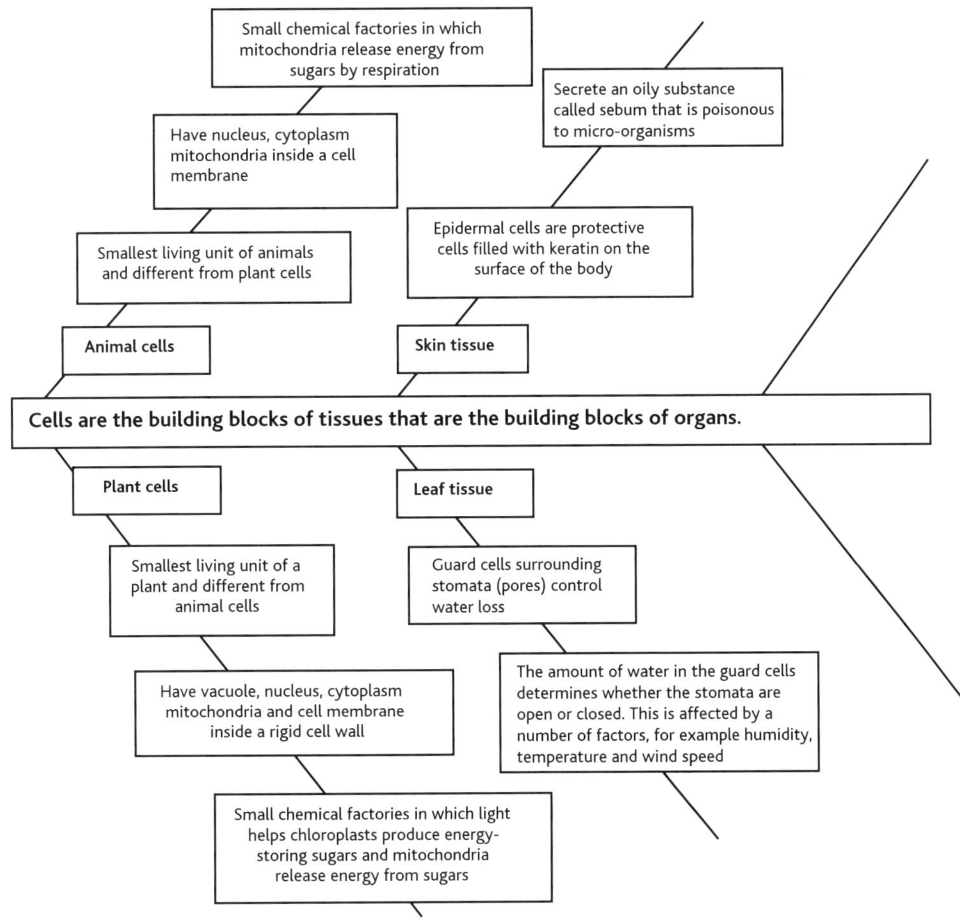

Figure 6.7 An example of a herring-bone diagram

A herring-bone diagram (Figure 6.7) is an effective way to organise information. It is used to describe events or relate concepts in terms of six questions:

- What is it?
- What does it do?
- How does it do it?
- When does it do it?
- Where does it do it?
- Why does it do it?

A sentence is composed as a backbone and the chains of concepts are drawn off from this sentence like ribs to form a herring-bone skeleton. It is a refined concept map that gives some sense to the lateral relationship of linked concepts. They are useful for the gifted student since they can summarise texts and materials and use them for revision purposes.

Flow charts

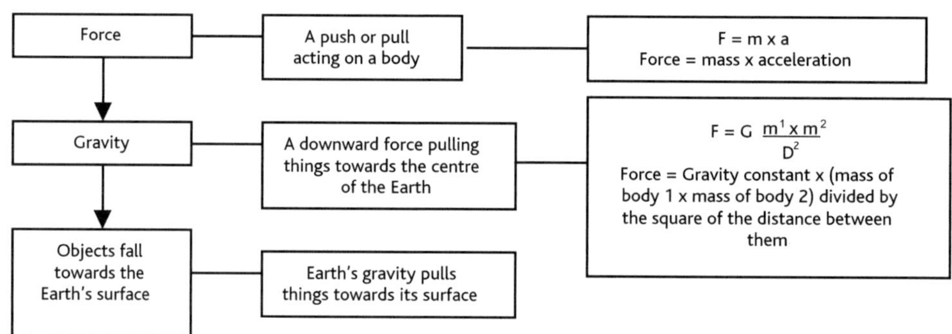

Figure 6.8 An example of a flow chart

A flow chart (Figure 6.8) is useful for organising spatial information, chronological information, cause and effect relationships, and process information.

Flash cards

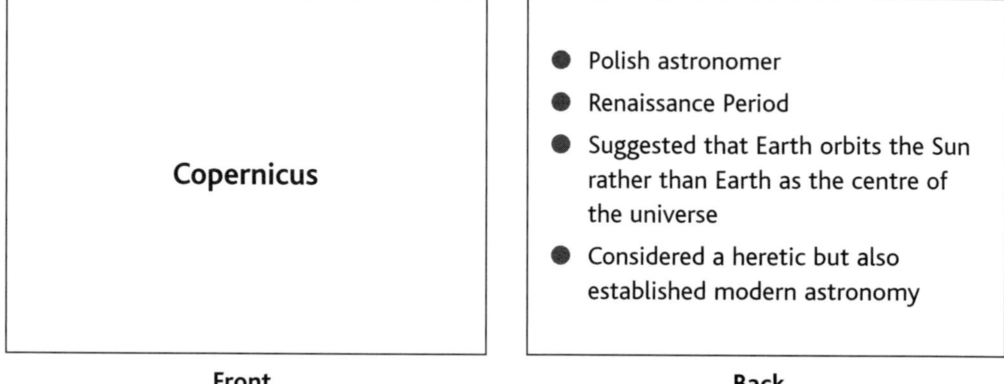

Figure 6.9 An example of a flash card

Flash cards are used to organise ideas and definitions, people and contributions, time periods and other types of information. When identifying major terms, people and concepts, focus on four things:

- Who or what is the term?
- With what is it associated?
- What is its function or purpose?
- Why is the term or concept important to the study of the subject?

An example of a flash card about Copernicus is shown in Figure 6.9.

Zones of relevance and mystery activities

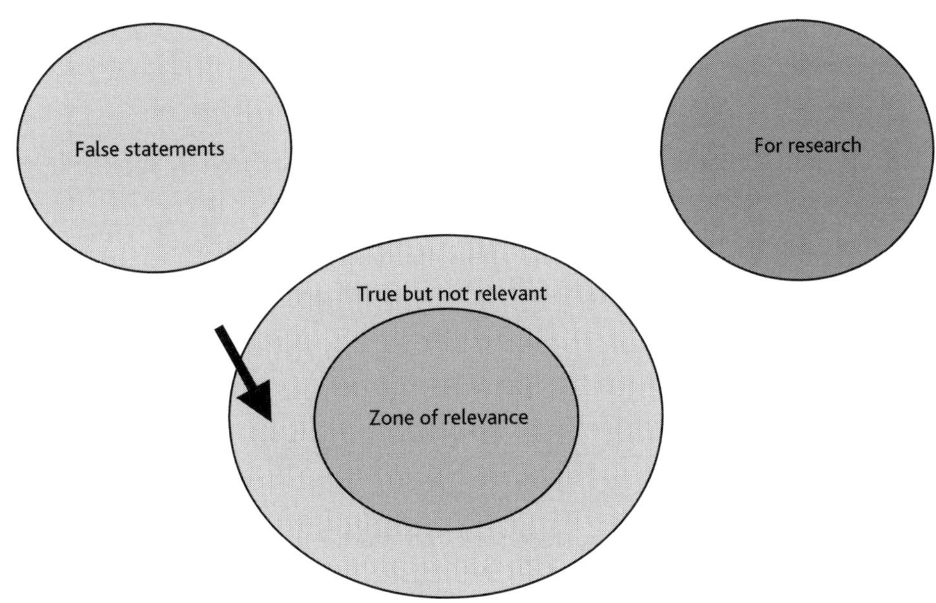

Figure 6.10 A zones of relevance and mystery diagram

Zones of relevance and mystery activities are activities with no clear outcome but a lot of evidence that needs sorting. The process starts by examining the evidence, data, descriptions or hypotheses in relation to an event or phenomenon, such as a list of statements relating to cells, animals and plants, and using the circles, arranged as shown in Figure 6.10, as collecting and focusing points for the statements.

The student sorts the statements into false, true, or don't know and need to research. The student then sorts the true statements into relevant or not relevant to the evidence, data, descriptions or hypotheses. If more than one hypothesis etc. are tested the relevant statements can be examined for key status, for example if the evidence supports three hypotheses then it can be considered as key information. These statements can then be gathered and written into continuous prose within a prescribed genre. Alternatively if data or descriptions are being examined then the student can be asked to provide a hypothesis to explain the data, event or phenomenon. The skills being developed are analysis and classification, concept understanding, explaining and justification. An example of the use of zones of relevance and mystery is an extension exercise on rocks, volcanoes, earthquakes and rock formation.

Example of a zone of relevance and mystery activity

Use the three following hypotheses separately and place all the cards that relate to each hypothesis in the different groups – False, Research, True and irrelevant or True and relevant (the zone of relevance). Start with the first hypothesis and then change the hypothesis and move the cards according to the new zone of relevance.

Hypothesis 1
The Earth consists of a sequence of layers:

(a) The crust is a thin rigid layer of fairly low density rock.
(b) The mantle is a very hot molten layer of high density rock that flows and creates currents of electrical charge and a magnetic field.
(c) The core is composed of two parts: a hot dense liquid of iron and nickel sloshing around because of the Earth's rotation; and an inner core of extremely hot iron under intense pressure so it is a solid.

Hypothesis 2
The Earth is made up of surface plates that move on the surface of a molten layer.

Hypothesis 3
The material of the mantle boils up and spills out onto the surface. Each rock sample has many tiny magnets in it that line up with the Earth's magnetic field. This is frozen into the solid rock.

Statements:

1. Drills have penetrated 12 kilometres of the Earth's surface.
2. The radius of the Earth is about 6,000 kilometres.
3. The combined density of all surface rocks on the Earth is 3.0 kg/m^3.
4. The density of the entire Earth globe is 5.4 kg/m^3.
5. Magnets have two poles – a north-seeking pole and a south-seeking pole.
6. A compass shows the true north of the Earth.
7. A magnet has a north and south pole.
8. Magnetic poles have remained static since the Earth was formed.
9. The Earth's magnetic field has changed many times over its existence.
10. Earthquakes occur randomly on the Earth's surface.
11. Volcanoes occur randomly over the Earth's surface.
12. Earthquakes and volcanoes occur in particular regions on the Earth's surface.
13. Earthquakes produce waves that can be felt in other parts of the Earth.
14. Some earthquake waves are not detected at a point directly opposite the earthquake.
15. Some earthquake waves are bent by the contents of the Earth.
16. The west coast of Africa fits with the east coast of South America.
17. The Earth is the same temperature all through.
18. The core of the Earth is very hot compared with the surface.
19. The central core of the Earth is a solid sphere of heavy metals.
20. Part of the Earth's rock surface is being destroyed by heat.

21. Part of the Earth's rock surface is being created by volcanic action.
22. Earthquakes are the result of movements in the Earth's core.
23. There are volcanoes at the bottom of the sea.
24. The American continent is moving away from the European continent.
25. The Himalayas are getting higher because India is crashing into Asia.
26. Earthquakes can be predicted.
27. The Chinese used small foreshocks to predict a big earthquake.
28. The geology of Earth is similar to the geology of other planets.
29. Other planets have volcanoes.
30. Other planets will have earthquakes.

Argument mapping

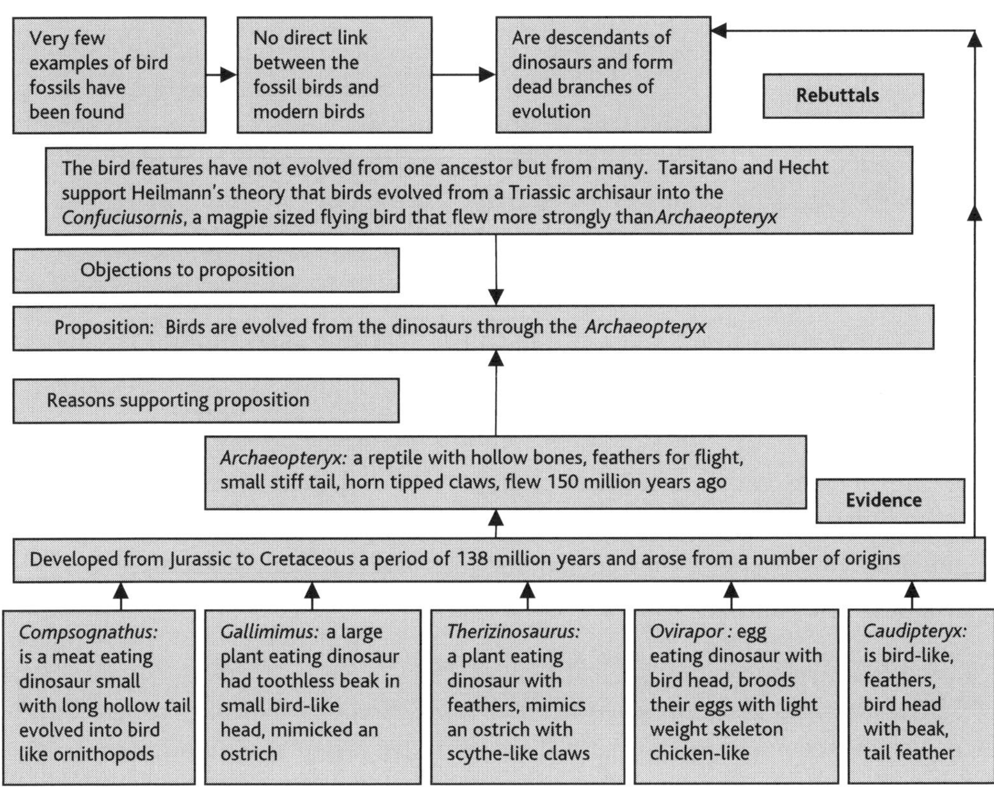

Figure 6.11 An example of argument mapping

Argument mapping is concerned with producing graphical 'boxes and arrows' maps of complex debates. The result is a paper chart presenting an overview of the reasoning. Argument mapping focuses on the inferential or evidential structure among claims and reasons to produce paper charts of the relationship of the factors contributing to an argument. Although similar to concept mapping and decision analysis, it is important to distinguish argument mapping from other techniques such as concept mapping and decision analysis as the example in Figure 6.11 shows.

Argument mapping expands an individual's capacity to grasp complex debates by presenting the argumentation in a two-dimensional spatial layout. Because it translates abstract conceptual structure into a simple spatial structure argument mapping is only really suitable for the gifted student and gives them the following:

- a permanent record of thinking on a topic that contributes to a debate;
- clarity and rigour in thinking by improving the sharing of knowledge in a group, leading to a deeper understanding of issues;
- extremely efficient ways to present overviews, indicating the boundaries of current knowledge or debate in complex argumentation to another student;
- better decision making by ensuring that a higher proportion of relevant considerations are taken into account.

Games

Games are good tools to help develop thinking skills in all abilities, but for the gifted the design of games which mimic the science models or conventions can be particularly productive in helping them consolidate their ideas and enabling students to learn difficult ideas in a fun situation, lessening the concept difficulty. Games can be revision aids and in simplifying complex concepts they allow access to complex areas of science and can be used as assessment techniques. The great gain with games is they aid attitude and affect effective learning because they offer:

- excitement with complex ideas sometimes using realistic situations;
- competition with one's peers and a need to understand the rules;
- promotion of longer and more sustained levels of concentration and motivation;
- participation and involvement in an act of learning but a feeling of enjoyment overriding the sense that one is learning.

To be effective the game must involve decision making so the student examines the ideas and the rationale for action. The best games are ones that promote:

- problem-solving approaches demanding high levels of communication;
- listening skills and high levels of cooperation;
- manipulation of complex ideas and applying them to situations.

Card games are generally classification style exercises that aid the learning of facts. The most common models are Happy Families, Snap and Rummy. Areas ideal for development are characteristics of the Periodic Table and properties of elements, types of electromagnetic waves, body parts of plants and animals, groups of organisms, adaptation, equations and reactions.

In the main matching and sorting games are easy for students to devise. For example Happy Families can be used for developing ideas about the Periodic Table or reactivity, organ systems and processes and cell types, while Snap can be used for concepts and words.

Equations can be turned into domino type games or collecting card games like Rummy where the player collects cards and so places a 'suit' on the table to enable them to write an equation or describe a process like photosynthesis or adaptation. In the example of adaptation each adaptation style for feeding, or running, or swimming, or protection of young etc. should be collected to display a suit relating to an animal or group of animals.

Board games are useful for developing a sense of the sequence in a cyclic process. These are based upon such games as Ludo, Snakes and Ladders or Monopoly. The ideas need to be cyclic processes and to promote flow in the game students should have access to information cards that can also contain inhibitors relating to negative feedback or stalls in the process. To promote probability chance cards can be added. Areas ideal for these approaches are carbon, water or nitrogen cycles, digestion, circulation, photosynthesis, respiration, oxidation, reduction, energy transfer, balanced forces, predator/prey and blood flow during exercise or rest, rock cycles and erosion.

Quiz games such as truth/untruth cards or *Who Wants to be a Millionaire?* with supports like 'Ask the audience', 'Ask a friend' or '50:50' are good for developing a sense of support and involvement. They can reveal depth of knowledge about a topic and can be used as a revision activity but the gifted can write questions for their peers. Quiz games can be adapted to 'What am I?' style games where a description is given, and 'Yes/No' questions asked and people must guess what it is. Another variant is where a card is pinned on the back of someone and each person has to give some information about the thing on the card without giving away the name or object. The person wearing the card has to guess what they are. These can be adapted for all abilities and coupled with a taboo in which certain words are banned they promote greater attention to thinking and language skills.

Probability games are good devices for developing an idea of genetics or any systems where chance is a possibility such as radioactivity. In this set of games the student spins a coin and allows the result to determine the characteristic. Two heads or a single head represent a dominant gene or decay process while a tail is a recessive gene. If a teacher is extending the curriculum for the gifted science student this approach offers a direct concrete model to allow the pupils to gain access to difficult ideas.

Under the heading of games we can group puzzles. These cover anagrams, word searches, crossword designing, jigsaws, code making and breaking, thinking and number exercises. They are designed to be stimulating exercises and develop a feel for the concepts to be covered and many gifted students enjoy designing them for themselves or others. They can also be a good starting point when extending the curriculum because they can consolidate the prior knowledge for access to the new topic by offering support for learning new concepts. They require the student to reflect and so are good for summarising and revision work. The danger is puzzles can become mechanical. They need to have an action that will require the student to do something with the material they have been puzzling over. They can also form the basis of interclass competitions promoting enthusiasm and excitement. Puzzles can be jigsaws to enable students to assimilate the structure of something like a cell or an organ system. While the student is concentrating on the relationship of the lines and patterns they are becoming familiar with visual clues that will help them to read a diagram or associate it with an idea. Or they can be a sequencing operation to develop some sense of the sequence of events in something like an energy transfer, a chemical reaction, an element cycle like the carbon or water cycle, life cycle, menstrual cycle, development of an organism etc.

CHAPTER 7

Implications for Teaching – Metacognition

The development of an individual's learning style will be influenced by the ease and comfort they experience in the learning situation. The level of security and confidence in one's skills affects the ability to gain success and will affect the student's emotional intelligence, self-esteem and motivation. For some gifted students this will be due to the frustration of a curriculum that seems to hold no cultural link for them; for others it will be imperfections in their reasoning capabilities.

Frustration in understanding what the expectations are in a science lesson or from the science curriculum can affect the student's metacognition. In some students where the verbal skills are not so well developed the metacognition is likely not to be expressed in a positive fashion. Some students develop a negative success pattern, that is failing in an activity to cause frustration in the teacher becomes a personal measure of success in a learning situation. The failure is recognised as a personal attainment leading to the reinforcement of self-belief in being a failure. This is often expressed as low self-esteem but with a high sense of street credibility since the recognition by one's peers is more important than success in the classroom.

The impression given in this situation is it is not 'cool' to be bright. Science teachers have to be clear about the relevance of the work to these students since they are very able to succeed but see a narrow horizon with regard to success. This will also require exposure to science in lots of exciting and novel contexts and contact with adults other than teachers to promote a positive role model.

This negativity can be seen in some Year 7 students from schools where control on the curriculum has not allowed the student free thought in science. Often there has been too much reliance by the teacher upon absolute right answers related to some sense of truth, or sometimes too much control on the student's thinking within a set paradigm. These students can find the probability nature of science a big challenge and need help to develop an awareness of this exciting characteristic of science.

Low esteem can also be seen in students who come from backgrounds where academic success is not the norm for the culture of the community or they are the first generation aspiring to high academic achievement. This tension between balancing their awareness of their ability with street credibility needs help from school and contact with successful students who come from the same background.

These low esteem gifted students may need other help to develop metacognition and a positive view of their learning and this can be achieved by asking them to evaluate their own learning using evaluation sheets and thinking logs.

An evaluation sheet would ask students to comment on:

- 'What have you learnt in the session or topic?'
- 'What posed the biggest challenge?'
- 'What was the most interesting aspect?'
- 'What would you have wished to have learnt more about?' and
- 'Which learning approach helped you the most?'

This puts the learning in a context of personal development and, if linked to a mentoring system and targets, can help the student measure their own progress. The thinking log does the same but is kept over a longer period of time to build a cumulative record.

CHAPTER 8

Implications for Teaching – Intelligence Traits and Learning Styles

Sternberg (1994) argues teachers must systematically vary teaching and learning to challenge and support the student's learning style. This calls for differing and more specific assessment methods to gain information about the thinking and learning styles of the students. Carbo and Hodges (1988) indicate in their work that: 'matching students' learning styles with appropriate learning strategies improves the ability of the student to concentrate and learn independently'.

If learning styles are not targeted specifically enough students who are mismatched will feel anxious and frustrated and some can show signs of physical illness. Sternberg reports that students whose learning style matches the teachers, will tend to attain higher levels of achievement. Teachers need to learn to be flexible and in their own teaching exhibit different styles in their classroom. In the planning of learning situations and activities teachers need to consider three factors:

- Creating a learning environment that is consistently **interesting** and **promotes curiosity**;
- Combining text with pictorial, visual and other interactive experiences such as ICT programs with groups engaged in Socratic discussions to help students **create and develop mental models and generalise** their experiences;
- Developing cognitive structures that allow students the **ability to bridge** their learning and unify their learning experiences.

Pogrow (1994)

This has a direct link to the methods identified as effective in the previous discussion on brain compatible learning. The mathematician Gregorc (1979) argues: 'The mind is the instrument by which and through which we interact with the world. It is *the* primary medium for the learning/teaching process.' In his work upon learning he recognises two continua that inform and allow learners to develop the distinctive learning styles and patterns of thinking in their learning. These continua are important when considering learning styles as factors in teaching for gifted students. In Gregorc's model one continuum relates to the way the learner perceives information (Figure 8.1) and the other relates to encoding, or the way the learner orders and stores the information (Figure 8.2). These continua are interactive with each other to give the learner a learning style that links perception to encoding. Gregorc took the interaction of learning perception and learning encoding to create four differing learning styles (Figure 8.3), which is very similar to that of Kolb (1984).

Figure 8.1 How we perceive information (Gregorc 1979)

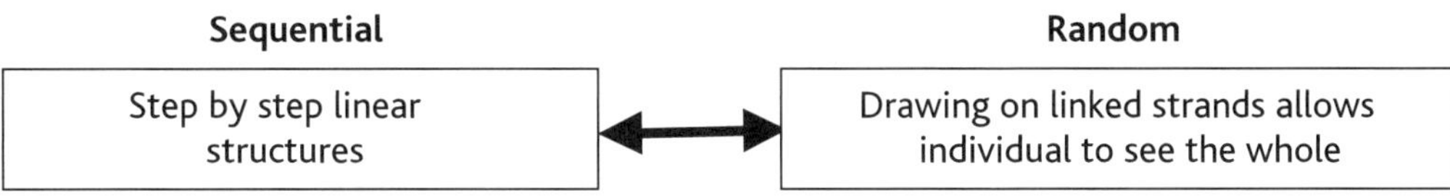

Figure 8.2 How we order and store information (Gregorc 1979)

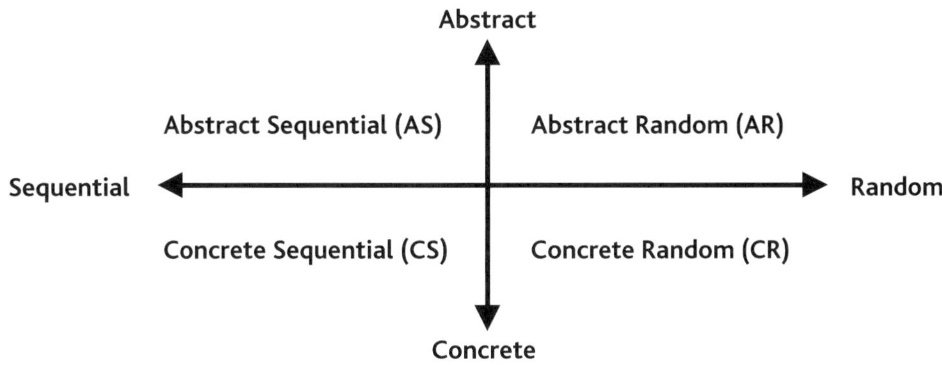

Figure 8.3 Four different learning styles (Gregorc 1979)

Gregorc (1984) argues that every individual can demonstrate the use of all four styles, but 95 per cent of the population will express a preference for one dominant style. Because of their metacognition gifted students are aware of their learning styles and some will be experimenters and eager to try different things; others will be very conservative and reluctant to attempt new approaches. Gregorc argues that strong correlations exist between the motivation and attitude of the individual, the activity and media being used for developing the learning and the teaching strategy being used by the teacher to facilitate learning. This will affect the reluctance or eagerness to try new approaches. The differences described can be seen in the following descriptions of the characteristics of each student type:

- **Abstract Sequential (AS)** learners are those whose skills are dominated with written, verbal and image symbols. They like to learn through reading, listening and using their verbal visual skills. They are highly verbal, using words as conceptual devices. They prefer a logical development to an argument and a sequential presentation that is rational and substantive or they consider it a waste of time. ASs can be highly sceptical individuals.
- **Abstract Random (AR)** learners have a capacity to free think and brainstorm. They enjoy an unstructured environment such as group discussions and investigational activities and use both verbal and visual mediums equally well.

They prefer not to be restricted by unnecessary rules and guidelines, in fact they enjoy experimenting with conventions. ARs often use hand and body movements when communicating. They dislike routine activities and cold, unemotional people.

- **Concrete Sequential (CS)** learners prefer direct, hands-on experiences. They exhibit good development of their five senses. They like touchable, concrete materials, orderly presentations and structured explorations. CSs actually enjoy formal lessons with short direct set experiments and demonstrations. They are adverse to free thinking or lessons without structure and desire perfection in their work.
- **Concrete Random (CR)** learners like to experiment using trial-and-error approaches, jumping to conclusions and preferring to work independently or in small groups of intrapersonal people. They are gamblers and risk takers, often arrive late and try to leave early if they feel the work is boring or going nowhere. They are leaders not followers, taking charge and being in charge and thriving in a competitive atmosphere. They refuse to accept the words 'don't' or 'can't' and are not overly concerned with making impressions or going out of their way to win over people. They are often the prime movers of change.

A number of teachers such as John Welham, Phil Plester and Chris McDonnell at Camborne School and Community College have used Gregorc work to good effect in a controlled style in the classroom. A number of science teachers and teachers of the gifted are beginning to take a deep interest in the link between learning styles and success since it seems to link closely with the work shown in the CAT learning style approach (O'Brien 2003). In this approach the style of materials used and thinking demand required to solve the problem are critical in helping to determine the learning style match of the student allowing them to achieve high attainment. Welham, Plester and McDonnell have commented upon their work on matching learning styles in the following way:

> Individuals with clear-cut dispositions toward concrete and sequential reality chose approaches such as ditto sheets, workbooks, computer-assisted instruction and kits. Individuals with strong abstract and random dispositions opted for television, movies and group discussion. Individuals with dominant abstract and sequential leanings preferred lectures, audiotapes and extensive reading assignments. Those with concrete and random dispositions were drawn to independent study, games and simulations. Individuals who demonstrated strength in multiple dispositions selected multiple forms of media and classroom approaches. It must be noted, however, that despite strong preferences, most individuals in the sample indicated a desire for a variety of approaches in order to avoid boredom.

Bob Burden (1998) is another to comment that a student's concept of themselves as a thinker and learner often correlates well with their IQ score and school achievement. Another similar approach to learning styles worth some attention is that of McCarthy (1982) – the 4MAT approach, which is similar to the above Gregorc model moving through a four-stage cycle for learning as follows:

Concrete experience to reflective observation
From practice and application to experimentation

All these approaches to examining thinking and learning style show there is a strong link between the nature of the activity, context and the thinking skill demand.

What keeps coming to the fore is Bloom's taxonomy (see Chapter 4) and an example of the use of this hierarchy for differentiation and considering learning style is given below (there is another example in Chapter 4).

Example of the use of hierarchy for differentiation

Challenge: Earthquakes

You are working as a group of researchers for a building company. You are working on earthquakes and have to supply them with details about earthquakes and the effects they have. To do that first you need to develop your own knowledge so each person in the group will research one of the following areas and then prepare a brief for each member in the team.

Student number 1 in the group should:

- Prepare a glossary by finding out the meanings of the following earth science words and prefixes. Identify which language do they come from?

Seismic	Tectonic	Tsunamis
Palaeo	Lithos	Epicentre

- Find out what are the following:

  Lithosphere
  Asthenosphere

  What part do they play in an earthquake event?

- Find a map of the world showing where earthquakes occur.
- Find out is there any pattern to the regions that experience Earthquakes? What is that pattern?

Student number 2 in the group should concentrate on researching:

- What is the cause of an earthquake and what are a focus and a fault?
- What are convection currents and how are a saucepan of gently boiling water and earthquakes related?
- Who were Giuseppe Mercalli and Charles F. Richter?
- How do we measure the intensity and magnitude of an earthquake?
- Where, when and what was the strength of the most recent earthquake?
- Which country has suffered the most earthquakes of Richter scale 7 since 1900?

Student number 3 in the group should concentrate on researching:

- What are S-, P-, and L-waves and which wave is first to reach a seismometer?
- How do we find the epicentre of an earthquake?
- How does a seismometer work and what does it measure?
- Why do scientists say the magnitude is measured on a logarithmic scale?
- Give reports of seismic events in Dudley 09.2002, Wakefield 09.2000 and Dogger Bank 06.1931.
- What is meant by a 'felt' report and what were they for Dudley or Wakefield in different areas of England?

Student number 4 in the group:

- You have a map showing the paleo-rock record for the African and American coastlines. Use this to study the relationship between the paleo-rock records on the American and African coast.

- Do you note any pattern in the shape and distribution of rocks and the distribution of fossils on adjacent continents?
- What is that pattern and explain how it could have occurred?
- What is the geology of the surface rocks at Long Lat. 140E, 43N and Long Lat. 5W, 56N?

Student number 5 in the group should concentrate on researching:

- What is a destructive and subduction zone also known as a converging plate boundary?
- What is the difference between a transform and compressional earthquake area also known as a strike-slip plate boundary and what is the relationship to rock faults?
- Investigate the building materials used in earthquake areas.
  - What are the best materials and design for buildings in an earthquake zone?
  - What are the best rocks to build on in an earthquake zone?

Now work as a group to discuss your brief and map the material onto a concept map.

Calculate the following and consider what evidence they supply to explain earthquakes.

Quake	Focus depth (km)	Distance of epicentre from coast (km)	Quake	Focus depth (km)	Distance of epicentre from coast (km)
A	–45	0	M	–50	90 east
B	–290	105 east	N	–310	485 east
C	–395	450 east	P	–485	290 east
D	–75	85 east	Q	–670	540 east
E	–120	245 east	R	–80	85 west
F	–190	60 east	S	–530	210 east
G	–685	410 east	T	–90	20 west
H	–15	45 east	U	–450	600 east
J	–510	685 east	V	–630	670 east
K	–525	385 east	W	–40	80 west
L	–400	345 east	X	–60	90 west

- Is there any relationship between distance from the coast to the epicentre and the depth of the earthquakes?
- Discuss and deduce if this is a converging plate boundary or a strike plate boundary. What is your evidence?
- Discuss and deduce if the continent is located east or west of the plate boundary. What is your evidence?
- Explain why earthquakes do not occur below 700 km.

Earthquakes produce a number of different waves that pass through the Earth at different speeds. Primary waves cause rock particles to move back and forth in the same direction as the wave is travelling, secondary waves cause rock particles to move at right angles to the direction of travel of the wave and surface waves cause the rock particles to move in a circular pattern. Primary waves travel at about 6.0 km/s and secondary waves travel at about 3.5 km/s. The third wave type, known as longitudinal or surface waves, travel at about 2.0 km/s. The following table gives a set of arrival times for primary and secondary waves travelling over different distances. Use the table to construct a line graph, use the *x* axis for the epicentre distance and *y* axis for travel time.

Distance from epicentre (km)	Travel times	
	Primary wave (min)	Secondary wave (min)
1000	2.5	4.5
2000	4.25	7.5
3000	5.75	10.0
4000	7.2	12.5
5000	8.5	15.0
6000	9.6	17.0
7000	10.7	19.0
8000	11.6	20.75
9000	12.5	22.2
10000	13.1	23.2

- What is the difference in arrival times for the following epicentre distance?
  a. 1000 b. 2250 c. 3000 d. 5000 e. 7500 f. 9500
- How could you use this information to calculate an epicentre?
- How many readings would you need to calculate the epicentre's position?

Gifted students use their awareness of thinking to maximise their learning strategies on a personal basis and, helped by their thinking traits or intelligences, they devise a number of techniques to assist their learning. Such techniques include: mnemonics relating to a sequence of text, words or numbers; rhythmic jingles to aid the learning of a sequence of facts or ideas; mind mapping to organise their knowledge; concept mapping to indicate links; and brainstorming to search for plausible ideas. All these approaches illustrate the creativity that these gifted science students have and teachers should adopt approaches to encourage creativity using as the definition:

> Creativity is the ability to play imagination games – thought experiments.

Tony Buzan (1993) observes that breakthroughs in science have often come about as a result of a dream, daydream, an accident, or a chance happening that moved the dreamer to diverge from the dominant paradigm.

In science there must be a conscious effort on behalf of the school to develop thinking strategies in science to prevent 'box' thinking and promote creativity in gifted science students. Techniques such as mysteries, taboo, games, etc. will work but often it will need more lateral thinking exercises such as those designed by de Bono (1989) to develop creativity. For example those shown in the box below.

Examples of lateral thinking exercises

Hypothesis, speculation and provocation

Why do you think mice have long tails? Put forward two different hypotheses and justify them.

OR

Because of genetic variations and environmental effects cows are being born very small. This is resulting in the large species of cow being quickly swamped and overtaken in numbers. What would be the consequences of this event?

Breadth of perception

In a genetic experiment there is an opportunity to redesign the human body. What things would be candidates for redesigning? Explain why they should be redesigned.

Alternatives, possibilities, choices

A mysterious disease strikes in the south-east area. It strikes quickly and is very contagious, so much so that everyone in contact with the disease becomes infected. Eventually 70 per cent of the working population catch the disease and 90 per cent are left severely deaf and lacking full speech faculties. Brainstorm what would be the effects of this affliction and how these effects could be overcome so the people could carry out all the functions of a modern society.

Consequence and sequel

A new medicine involving some genetic engineering is discovered that will allow people to live to the age of 120 years. This medicine is expensive and has not been trialled over a period longer than the statutory seven years. What are the consequences and sequel on the immediate use of such a drug without control? What could be the long-term implications if its use is controlled?

Teachers can develop thinking in all students by their questioning by concentrating upon the following progression of questions, but for the gifted it is the speculative nature of correlational and synthesis style questions that promotes creativity:

- **Observation** – 'What do you see?' 'Look carefully, describe how it happens.'
- **Prediction** – 'What will happen if... ?' 'What's the next thing to happen when... ?'
- **Causal reasoning** – 'This happens because... happened.' 'If you do this then... will happen.'
- **Application** – 'If we consider this problem...' 'What do you think will be the important thing to do to make... happen?'
- **Correlational reasoning** – 'It could be... are connected and so... will happen and... will change by...' 'These two factors could be connected.'
- **Synthesis** – 'What would you want to investigate to explore this problem?'
- **Evaluation** – 'What would be the consequence of that event?' 'Would it happen every time or are there other conditions which help it to happen?'

CHAPTER 9

Implications for Teaching – Context, Role, Language and Content

Learning is strongly affected by the context in which the learning is placed, the role the student is expected to play in the context for learning and the relationship of the content to the context and role. Context is concerned with the relationship of the domains of knowledge affecting the solution and the transfer of cognitive skills to solve problems. Although gifted children may appear more capable, they will have differential levels of ability in different knowledge domains and one of the most common variables is that of verbal reasoning skills, which directly affects their ability to read and write. In considering context as an enrichment tool it is not just the physical situation in which the knowledge or concepts are set, but also the framework of the text that will affect the degree of challenge for the student.

Because text is the product of thinking, it carries a social aspect from the originating person that is exchanged when the receiving individual decodes it. Halliday and Hasan (1980) identify text as an expression of meaning and logic in which a semantic or unit of meaning is both a product of and a process for thinking and interpreting. The social aspect is a vital part of the context, which Halliday and Hasan define as having three features:

- Field – what is happening – the nature of the action;
- Tenor – who is taking part, their status, role and relationship;
- Mode – the part language plays, the symbolic organisation of the text.

In any subject it is not just the context to be considered but the words and in a subject like science the words become more specific in depth and meaning, thus they become conceptual devices for communication. For the student to communicate effectively they must have a level of understanding of the concept and language to be used to indicate the real meaning of the science.

Bellack *et al.* (1966) observed the classroom as a context in which teachers and students played games with the process of learning. They identify the teacher as the active player, the one who makes the most moves, speaks most frequently and longest. The major part of the game is played with structures determined and defined by the teacher. Fact stating and explaining is often more frequent than defining and interpreting.

Opinions and the justification of them are relatively rare and the teacher frequently acts like a solicitor, the student a respondent. In a number of science lessons this is a common statement of action and the student is relatively passive as a learner. Work in science offers all students many opportunities to develop all aspects of their communication skills and also acts as a differentiating tool for the gifted student. For example:

- Dealing with ideas means using science language to transmit ideas in a written or symbolic form once the model representation is developed.
- Listening to others talk about science and making sense of the language requires a good command and range of words and their meanings. It is the ability to understand the use of science words in context that allows us to challenge and reflect upon our own science ideas.
- Reading about science ideas helps one to reflect upon one's own ideas and helps to challenge one's thinking and give breadth to our understanding of a science idea in different contexts.
- Analysing science information and interpreting data to arrive at a conclusion and then to evaluate the conclusion in conjunction with the original idea requires an accuracy of science language and vocabulary to enable the student to become precise and accurate in their communications.

It must be remembered that communication is not, by definition, a solitary activity and involves working with others, so in science group work is an important consideration in the design of an activity to develop effective communication. This implies the student needs to have knowledge of their role as communicator and the audience they are writing for. As Button (1983) stated: 'To be human is synonymous with being in communication and relationship with other people, which demands of us a range of social skills.'

In her discussion of the role of language in science Bulman (1985) goes further and states language is not used just for educating students about science but to *educate students through science*. Science is envisaged as a vehicle to allow students to learn communication skills within a context that fascinates and excites them. For the gifted the implication of this is they should be challenged by higher level demands of language skills and vocabulary. It would also imply the demand of a balance between reading, writing, talking and listening activities in science.

However a number of surveys identify the total reading in science at Year 7 as varying between 8 and 10% of the whole activity and the major reading activity usually lasts only half a minute to one and a half minutes and concentrates on sentences or short passages. Further, presented text materials in science are often short, explicit explanations related to visual examples, that are frequently disjointed, undemanding or unexciting and for the gifted student this presents no challenge because it does not present the information in such a way that the student can construct and speculate on meaning. The picture improves by Year 10 where the quantity of reading rises to 10–12 % and there are more resources relating to issues in science that can offer more room for speculation and reconstruction but, in all key stages, the time for literacy activities is still often too low. This is particularly unhelpful for some gifted students because it denies them the opportunity to research for themselves.

Science Web Readers (Solomon 2000) advance a departure from the single textbook reader, presenting three readers for average to gifted audiences, offering different science contexts to develop ideas and present the student with context enrichment. They use the following basic strategy to develop active reading:

- Read to understand the ideas in the text; — **Read text**
- Compare the ideas with others you know;
- Highlight those that are relevant and new; — **Make notes**
- Reflect on those ideas; and
- Revise your ideas in light of what you have read. — **Apply ideas**

Wellington and Osborne (2001) identify the conceptual difficulties language can cause a student in science and argue it becomes easier to understand the difficulties and develop solutions to support the student if language development in science is viewed as a set of levels of comprehension. Wellington and Osborne view the levels of comprehension as shown in Figure 9.1.

Level 1 – These are **labelling words** or **nouns** that relate to tangible things or entities in science, e.g. plant, animal, vertebra, pollen, fulcrum, meniscus, saliva etc.

Some are new words for new things or nomenclature and are generally easy to learn in a science context, e.g. chemical elements, science laboratory, microscope, chemistry, cell, membrane, enzyme, haemoglobin, pathogen, compound, electromagnet, spectrum.

Some are new words for familiar things e.g. gut = oesophagus, backbone = vertebrae.

↓

Level 2 – These are **descriptive words** that become **nouns for process** events in science that are observable or demonstrable by practice.

These words can be defined by an action. Light a candle and the burning is described as combustion; separating sand from salt by using filter paper is described as filtration; plants making food using the sun demonstrated by the presence or absence of starch in a leaf exposed to light or dark is described as photosynthesis.

↓

Level 3 – These are **concepts** and represent a level of abstraction because they need other words and a context to make them understandable.

Some words are difficult to understand because they are derived from the experience of examples – so called sensory concepts, e.g. red is experienced from the interaction with colour (no experience, no concept), force is experienced as movement.

Some words are difficult to understand because they are theoretical constructions and often require models to explain them. The student must first have experience of a model to gain experience of the concept, e.g. mixture, compound, atom, electron, ion, field etc. Experience of the model develops a mental construct for understanding the concept.

Some have dual meanings. One in everyday and one in science, e.g. work, energy, mass, weight, power, fruit, salt. Needs discussion in context and frequent defining pictorially.

↓

Level 4 – This is the algebraic level of symbols and mathematical words and is derived from abstract theory such as mathematics or a model. It is independent of everyday experience.

This level requires a confidence in the other levels of science language to give it meaning.

Figure 9.1 The levels of comprehension (Wellington and Osborne 2001)

Teachers use an understanding of these levels to differentiate the work for less able students but they can be used to increase the level of demand for the gifted science student. Giving gifted science students a high level science text and getting them to simplify the material for a younger age group without losing any of the meaning can be an effective way of using these levels. It works because effective readers can move deftly through the levels of comprehension and show understanding by reinterpreting and describing the same thing in a number of different ways.

Therefore when an accomplished reader reads a text they interpret conceptual meaning showing they can use words and language as a tool for thinking. This can be used to develop the curriculum for the gifted by examining language in science. Clive Sutton (1992) looked at the interplay of language and meaning in science and describes a way the words themselves can be used to convey meaning. This is achieved by developing a consideration of the relationship of the word structure to the description of meaning embodied in the word. He envisages a word in the same way one would a fossil: the skeleton is present and gives a hint of meaning, likewise the word is a fossil of past ideas. This can be used to develop higher level homework by asking students to search for word origins as in the following example:

Dissolve: combination of the Latin *dis* meaning 'apart' and *solvere* meaning 'release' or 'loosen'

Good communication skills are important to allow gifted students to function in groups and ultimately in society. To assist the development of the gifted science student's communication skills science teachers should follow the guidelines in the box below.

Development of communication skills in science

- Develop the range and meanings of words by encouraging personal glossary work, including word origins and links with other ideas in science by the use of concept maps coupled with definitions.
- Encourage good content and effective organisation by developing thinking pads or storyboarding in which bullet points record ideas or phrases and help with the planning followed by the organisation of these into prose.
- Improve clarity by encouraging students to read their work aloud in small groups and to critically analyse the arguments being advanced and evaluate the effectiveness of communication.
- Expand the range of styles and genres by directing the writing into different forms, sharing good examples of other styles and forms and using them for critical activities. The results of this work should be exhibited around the school and in public places like libraries, shopping areas and museums.
- Further develop the imagery, irony, awareness and humour by using analogy and metaphor approaches to secure modelling skills and encourage students to discuss these in groups.
- Develop the skills of debate by using thinking pad exercises like argument maps, consequence maps, concept maps, mind maps, etc.
- Encourage the skills of editing and redrafting by giving students completed texts and asking them to redraft them according to different criteria and different audiences. For example for a newspaper piece for *The Times*, change the same article for the *Sun* or

Mirror, or write articles for a textbook or an encyclopaedia, or produce accurate science-fiction work such as diaries.

- Extend the range and creativity of communication by asking students to communicate ideas in different forms, for example music, song, poetry, dance, drama.
- Use other languages for writing or translating from, to develop an awareness of the structure of language.

Gifted science students can be encouraged to improve their reading and writing skills and make more effective use of texts to learn. However great care has to be taken here since this can be an area of great difficulty to some gifted students who have not developed their verbal skills to the same level as their other cognitive skills.

Choice of science textbooks for the gifted should be approached carefully since most textbooks present the subject as ready-made knowledge. A reader learns to manipulate meaning in relation to experience and ability, illustrating the importance of cognition and literacy skills. Hence any simple reading of a text gives the student little opportunity to reconstruct the knowledge for him or herself. This is because the information is presented as statements of fact and often all uncertainty has been removed from the text and the absolute replaces the speculative. Likewise the descriptive powers of a process word like 'filter', 'condense', 'diffuse' or 'decompose' are reduced to a narrow definition because they become nouns or clearly defined concepts. The student is faced with a choice:

'Do I accept this knowledge and learn it?'
Or
'Do I model with this knowledge and use it to describe an event?'

An effective and active gifted science student, who is secure in their verbal skills, can make the decision to use the knowledge and become an effective communicator both in written and in spoken language, but they need the examples to enable them to model their own skills. This is because the effective and active reader learns to:

- see underlying ideas in the text and discuss them, not just read the words, to change their views;
- pick out what is essential and new knowledge and compare ideas with what they already know;
- challenge ideas and revise their own mental models accordingly.

If verbal reasoning skills are not secure the student will find the above difficult and any speculation within the reading is quite forbidding because they have to rely on their own weak understanding of the text. This means the gifted science student who is secure in their verbal skills needs exposure to a range of science texts outside the key stage textbook and should be directed to other books in the school library to read on science. Such a reading list linked to the National Curriculum Science programmes of study could include the following.

Suggested reading list linked to National Curriculum programmes of study

History/culture of science:

- *Horrible Science* series – *Suffering Scientists* – Nick Arnold
- *Horrible Science* series – *Explosive Experiments* – Nick Arnold
- *Brief History of Time* – Editor John Gribben
- *The Big Idea* series – *Archimedes and the Fulcrum* – Paul Strathern
- *The Big Idea* series – *Crick, Watson and DNA* – Paul Strathern
- *The Big Idea* series – *Newton and Gravity* – Paul Strathern
- *Galileo's Finger* – Peter Atkins
- *Galileo's Commandment* – Editor Edmund Blair Bolles
- *The Biggest Ideas in Science* – Charles Wynn and Arthur Wiggins
- *Greatest Feuds of Science* – Hal Hellman
- *History of Medicine* – Editor Paul Lewis
- *The Dinosaur Hunters* – Deborah Cadbury
- *Rachel Carson: Witness for nature* – Linda Lear
- *Isaac Newton: The last sorcerer* – Michael White
- *Darwin and the Barnacle* – Rebecca Stott
- *Mendeleyev's Dream* – Paul Strathern
- *Mauve* – Simon Garfield
- *The Map That Changed the World* – Simon Winchester
- *Count Rumford: The extraordinary life of a scientific genius* – G.I. Brown

General ideas of science

- *Big Numbers* – Mary and John Gribben
- *The Unnatural Nature of Science* – Lewis Wolpert
- *Can Reindeer Fly: The science of Christmas* – Roger Highfield
- *The Science of Discworld* – Terry Pratchett, Ian Stewart and Jack Cohen
- *Foul Facts: Science – The Awful Truth* – Martyn Hamer and Jamie Stokes

Biology

- *Horrible Science* series – *Ugly Bugs* – Nick Arnold
- *Horrible Science* series – *Blood, Bones and Body* series – Nick Arnold
- *Horrible Science* series – *Nasty Nature* – Nick Arnold
- *Horrible Science* series – *Disgusting Digestion* – Nick Arnold
- *Horrible Science* series – *Evolve or Die* – Nick Arnold
- *Horrible Science* series – *Bulging Brains* – Nick Arnold
- *Dorling Kindersley Nature Encyclopaedia in association with Natural History Museum*
- *The Hidden Powers of Animals* – Dr Karl P. N. Shuker
- *Plague's Progress* – Arno Karlen
- *The Viking Atlas of Evolution* – Roger Osbourne and Michael Benton
- *Walking with Dinosaurs* – Tim Haines
- *Walking with Dinosaurs: How did they know that* – Dave Martill and Darren Nash

Chemistry

- *Horrible Science* series – *Chemical Chaos* – Nick Arnold
- *Elements of Chemistry* – Lavosier Translated by Robert Kerr
- *Molecules at An Exhibition* – John Emsley
- *The Chemical Elements* – Nechaev and Jenkins
- *Salt: A World History* – Mark Kurlansky
- *Crime Scene to Court* – Editor Peter White
- *Savage Earth: The dramatic story of volcanoes and earthquakes* – Alwyn Scarth
- *The Secret Life of Dust* – Hannah Holmes
- *Horrible Geography – Violent Volcanoes* – Anita Ganeri

Physics

- *Measuring the Universe* – Kitty Ferguson
- *Light Years* – Brian Clegg
- *Seeing and Believing* – Richard Panek
- *How the Universe Works* – Heather Couper and Nigel Henbest
- *The Way The Universe Works* – Robin Kerrod and Giles Sparrow
- *The Time and Space of Uncle Albert* – Russell Stannard
- *Uncle Albert and the Quantum Quest* – Russell Stannard
- *Black Holes and Uncle Albert* – Russell Stannard
- *Horrible Science* series – *Fatal Forces* – Nick Arnold
- *Horrible Science* series – *Sounds Awful* – Nick Arnold
- *Horrible Science* series – *Frightening Light* – Nick Arnold

The types of activities that develop better reading skills in students are active; they involve reflection, restructuring and discussion of and/or about words and text that are important for the development of language and range of vocabulary

As a consequence of poor reading skills some gifted science students can find non-fiction writing, particularly accurate writing in science, difficult because of the accurate science and formal structures demanded. The linguistic features of writing are difficult to understand because they go through the following lines of logic:

- First they need to identify the general and science language or vocabulary they wish to use to convey the science ideas.
- They need to write these and connect them using suitable connective words or phrases.
- The prose will need to be cohesive with respect to tense, action and development of the appropriate science idea.
- Finally, there is the act of writing the science information into an appropriate style or register for the material for a predetermined audience.

For gifted science students who experience weak verbal skills with regard to writing and understanding text and continuous prose, writing and reading in science are the most daunting aspects of their work and these gifted students use strong avoidance strategies to attempt to avoid this task. Flower and Hayes (1980) identify writing as a product and problem of reasoned thinking processes involving the use of mental models. The product of the process relies heavily upon:

- the writer's knowledge about the topic being written about, which determines the language and concepts;
- the context that directs the style/type or genre of writing, the audience that determines the level of language;
- the writer's knowledge of the processes and conventions of writing or schemata for writing that directs how the above can be put together to produce the product.

Flower and Hayes identify the process of writing as a complex one requiring the writer to: use information from the environment about the topic, role, audience and the purpose for writing; form new knowledge about the topic in symbolic form; and use knowledge from our long-term memory about information known about the topic and how to write in a reasoning pattern for the identified group. The use of mental models to reason patterns or schemata produces the written product as a function of our immediate working memory. This can be pictured as shown in Figure 9.2.

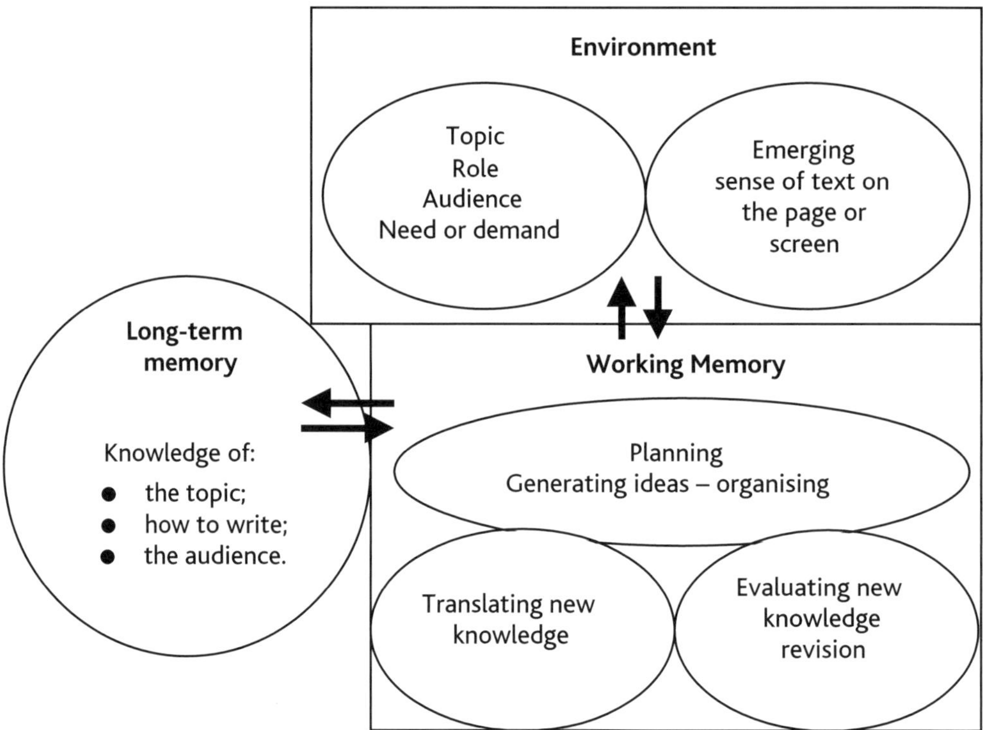

Figure 9.2 The written product – a function of environment, working and long-term memory (adapted from Flower and Hayes 1980)

In the working memory the writer is planning their science writing by generating and organising science ideas in relation to the target audience and purpose. To facilitate the process, science knowledge must be translated into accepted codes for the target audience; this is the drafting process. The draft writing is then reviewed by evaluating how well the material meets the criteria of the audience and the genre conventions and finally it is revised to produce the final prose.

Weak gifted students can learn to become more effective writers by talking about what they are going to write, whom they are writing for and what role they are assuming for the task of writing and using this process to plan their writing.

At this time they can use storyboarding to visually record their ideas and then learn to bullet point the main ideas and key words. In this process the handwriting is important because someone else will need to read the notes, but the level of correct grammar is not so important since it is the ideas that need to be developed.

The bullet pointed list is the basis of planning the flow of the text. It is at this point either teacher or student decides the genre of the writing, which may be one of the following:

- Recount;
- Report;
- Explanation;
- Procedural;
- Persuasion;
- Discussion.

It is also now that the use of a framework is discussed to help the student see the main structural points of the genre. The teacher discusses the material to be written into the writing frame. This is the translation or composition stage during which the teacher talks through the forming of sentences by vocalising aloud the sentence construction from the bullet points. In this process the student, supported by the teacher, identifies the time scale and indicates the tense of the writing followed by the drafting of the sentences into continuous prose so the cohesion of the text is maintained. If the writing and reading is to be successful and enjoyed by the gifted student it needs to be taught as a process with the following principles:

1. Writing should be recursive with each repeated action one of revision and redrafting. This allows the student an opportunity to reflect and restate their ideas. They need support to learn to write in different genres using 'writing frameworks' or 'storyboarding'. In both these the student is supported and able to produce a finished piece that cites his or her own ideas.
2. Writing should be shared with discussion about the content and the ways of expressing ideas. Time for discussion about the way it can be presented with effect allows the poor writer time to think and learn from others about different forms of writing.
3. Once the written work is complete it should be kept alive by being read and talked about. This will involve the students in criticism and evaluation.

Supported activities for reading and writing

Careful use of frameworks, brainstorms and other discussion techniques to assist reading and writing can help the gifted science student with verbal weaknesses work within a supportive structure and learn how to communicate effectively. Frameworks are context dependent so they should be taught in class work in science and not used as isolated skills. Other supportive activities are:

Word lists

Word lists are a powerful way of developing an awareness of the range of vocabulary in a subject. They generally are identified as the key words and in certain circumstances gifted students can be asked to identify the key words after reading a representative text relating to a topic. Word lists must be made to work and can be easily linked with other techniques such as **word links** or **concept maps** and **definitions** or **progressive glossaries**. Words should always be written in lower case but large font so the shape of the word is not compromised and students learn to associate the shape with the word. An example of a word list identified by a student is shown in Table 9.1.

Table 9.1 Word list identified by a student in biology

Key words	Dictionary definition	Pictorial representation
Vertebrate		
Invertebrate		
Mammal		
Amphibian		
Segment		
Abdomen		
Skeleton		
Exoskeleton		
Taxonomic group		
Characteristic		
Classify		
Inherited		
Environmental		
Variation		

To extend the task the student can be asked to link the words to a classification activity such as shown in Figure 9.3.

Words associated with features of the organism
Words associated with classification
Words associated with variation
Words to do with adaptation

Figure 9.3 Linking words to a classification activity

Progressive glossaries

Progressive glossaries are lists of linked words with visual representation that show the developing depths of meaning in words related to a topic. They are not arranged alphabetically because that would remove the organic links. For the gifted they can help develop an understanding of complex ideas and concepts. For example a progressive glossary would look like this:

- Particle – smallest bit of a material
- Atom – smallest bit of matter
  - Electron – negative particle in the atom orbiting the nucleus
  - Nucleus – small particle at the centre of the atom containing:
    - Proton – positive particle in the nucleus
    - Neutron – neutral particle in the nucleus
- Molecule – smallest bit of matter such as carbon based compounds
- Ion – smallest bit of matter such as metal salts
- Quarks – smallest bits of the atom

Drawing and bullet pointing

Drawing and bullet pointing is an activity in which the student draws a pictorial representation of their ideas and bullet points key ideas and words with the drawing. This safeguards the idea in a form that the student can work with. They go back over the pictures and bullet point descriptions and add time scale indicators. These bullet points are turned into sentences. The sentences are linked into paragraphs and the time indicators are used to tense the work. This allows the student to learn the process of planning the writing and the gifted student can also use it as a thinking pad to aid logic thinking. Figure 9.4 shows an example of drawing and bullet pointing.

- Light is white
- From a bulb
- Glass prism
- A triangle prism

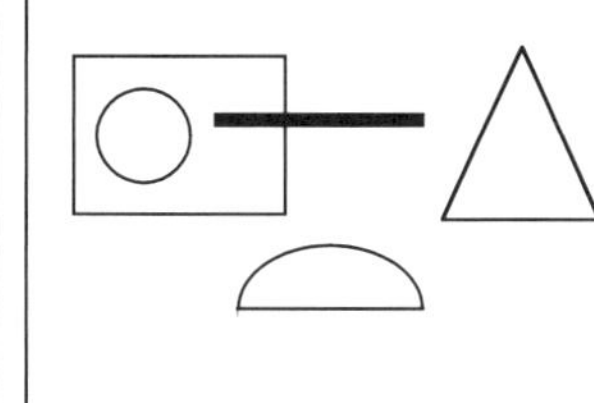

- Light from ray box
- Light comes out of thin slit
- Light in a straight line
- Light hits prism at angle
- Light ray

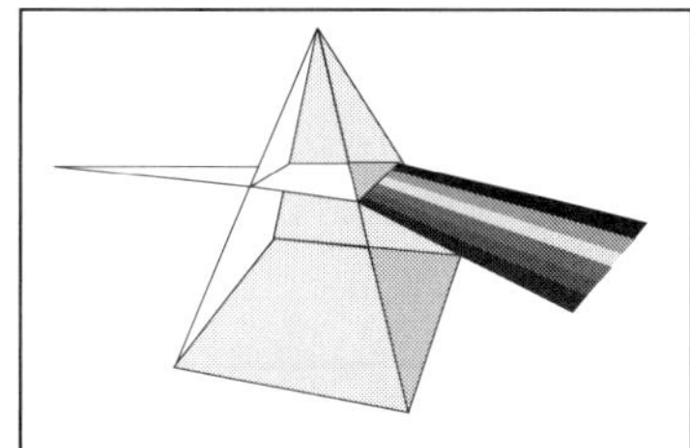

- Light passes through prism
- Light beam is bent
- Light is bent and split
- Bent = refraction
- White light split – ROY G BIV
- Spectrum formed

Figure 9.4 An example of drawing and bullet pointing

The bullet points shown in Figure 9.4 become the following sentences:

- White light comes from an electric bulb.
- A triangle block of glass is a prism.
- The light bulb is put inside a box with a slit in one side.
- The light comes out of the thin slit in a straight line called a ray.
- The light hits the side of the prism and passes through the prism.
- The light ray is bent or refracted and the white light splits into seven different colours.
- The colours are red, orange, yellow, green, blue, indigo and violet and this is called a spectrum.

The student changes this into:

> An electric bulb produces white light, which can be split by a glass prism into a spectrum.
>
> To do this a ray box is used. This consists of a black box with a bulb inside and a thin slit in one side. The light comes out of the thin slit as a straight beam or ray of light. The light ray hits the side of a prism, passes through the glass side and is bent or refracted. Because light consists of different coloured light not all the colours are bent the same amount. This splits the white light up so we see colours. The colours are red, orange, yellow, green, blue, indigo and violet. This is called a spectrum. We can remember the colours by ROY G BIV or by Richard of York gave battle in vain.

Sequencing

Sequencing is a powerful technique for determining understanding. A text is broken up into representative parts and the student must reconstruct the sentence or passage so it makes sense in terms of process, description and time scale.

Pictograms

Although the transmission of knowledge with pictograms could be deemed to be low, they are fun. They are motivating and when coupled with other work such as concept building they can help students with limited vocabularies and dyslexic students to build language. For the gifted they aid the clarification of processes and can be great revision aids.

Cloze activities

Cloze activities are predicting exercises that determine whether the student understands the text. They will work well for the gifted if all sentences have each fourth, fifth, or multiples thereof, words missing so allowing the student an opportunity to speculate on the meaning of a text. Cloze activities are good for developing basic study techniques, giving students an opportunity to make decisions, promote group discussions and speculate. Try not to overuse cloze activities; it is better to use cloze activities with a drawing exercise to help visually orientated students gain some access to the work.

Diagram completion and labelling

Diagram completion and labelling are powerful recording and comprehension techniques requiring students to more than copy a diagram from a book or the board. The student is asked to read a piece of text and use that text to add labels to the diagram or complete a section of the diagram, so they must understand what the diagram and text is about. Some students will have a difficulty in understanding two-dimensional representations of three-dimensional objects so these exercises need some careful designing but can be good diagnostic tools. Use of colour to link related parts could make the task more analytical. These exercises are good for the gifted students to help develop a sense of relationships between visual representations and text descriptions.

Collecting and sorting information

Collecting and sorting information at its simplest is a library search from either books or CD-ROMs. This is frequently left too open ended and teachers need to search the library or Internet first to identify the range of books and websites that a student could use to research information. This information should be given to the librarian with directions for these to remain in the library and a list of websites kept in an envelope that students sign for and open at the librarian's desk so giving all students an opportunity to research. This can be linked to active library skill development by using the library cataloguing system such as Dewy Nos. The questions the gifted student must answer should be open ended, with a limiting page or word count and a genre for reporting to be used to ensure the student does not just copy pages of material.

Sorting pictures and texts

Sorting pictures and texts is an extension of sorting and sequencing. The student is given a mixed sequence of photos and diagrams and text with one or more important sections missed out. They need to sort them into order and then link them by writing or drawing the missing bits into a complete piece of prose. Such exercises are good for gifted students when dealing with extended topics since they can help students gain access to difficult ideas based upon prior knowledge.

True/false statement sorting

True/false statement sorting is a decision-making process in which the student makes decisions about the correctness of statements describing an event. This gives them opportunity to examine the conceptual language of a science situation. It is better to get the students to reconstruct the statements into prose or a series of pictorial actions. This makes the gifted student interact by making more decisions about the representation of the action and concepts. An example of true/false statement sorting is shown in Table 9.2.

Table 9.2 An example of true/false statement sorting

Debs has dropped a bottle of lemon juice into a bowl of wet cake mix. The bottle has broken allowing the lemon juice to mix with the wet cake mix and now there is a lot of effervescence from the cake mix.

Statement	True	False	Don't know
The reaction is a chemical reaction and there will be new substances formed in the bowl.			
Effervescence means to put acid with alkali and make a salt.			
Effervescence means the fizzing that shows a gas is being released in a chemical reaction.			
Lemon is an acid.			
Lemon is an alkali.			
The effervescence came from the reaction of acid with a carbonate.			
The reaction of an acid with a carbonate releases carbon dioxide gas and an alkali.			
The cake mix is really a compound because the water has joined it together.			
Acid reacts with a carbonate to release carbon dioxide and water.			
The carbonate compound is found in the flour/baking powder mixture.			

Now take true statements and write them into a series of cartoons for a textbook for primary children describing what happened when Debs dropped the lemon juice into the cake mix.

Devising questions

Devising questions is a reverse comprehension activity where students are given a text and asked to construct questions on important ideas, concepts, models or diagrams. These are then exchanged between groups and the students answer the questions then hand them back for marking and comment. The answers are not just left but are open for debate with the teacher acting as arbitrator. An alternative for the gifted student is **'The answer is... What is the question?'**. In this approach the groups of students are given the answers and asked to devise the questions to accompany the answers. The question must show scientific accuracy and creativity so the answers need to be open ended to allow flexibility.

Graphic outlining

Graphic outlining is an analysis technique that links reading and writing. Readers need to construct meaning from the words on the page which requires them to interact with the text by interpreting it. Readers learn to skim the text, note the headings and illustrations/diagrams or data. They scan the piece, underlining key words and phrases, then read the piece carefully. Then using mind mapping they map the relationship and organisation of the knowledge in the text. It is a good revision tool to help students recall ideas.

Graphic outlining can be achieved by using the following steps:

1. Draw up three columns.
2. In the left-hand column list headings. Space them in proportion to the length of the section.
3. In the central column list sub-headings next to the main headings that they correspond to.
4. In the last column list illustrations, diagrams and data against sub-headings they correspond to.
5. Link them by lines and this gives you the graphic outline (see Figure 9.5).

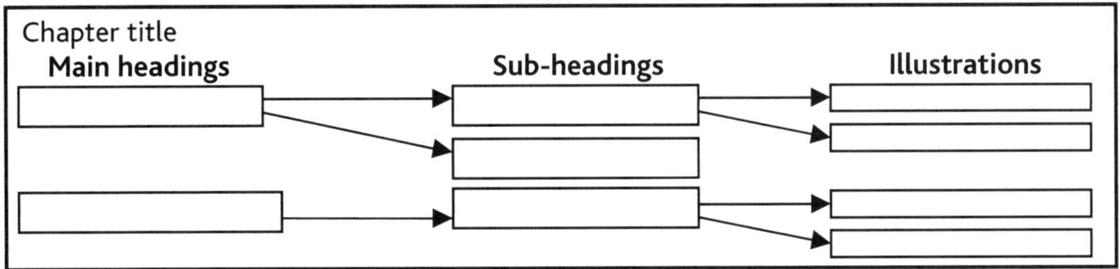

Figure 9.5 An example of graphic outlining

Text grids

A text grid is a research aid that helps students make notes for writing. It is a framework that helps them to organise information and link it to supporting alternative sources, as shown by the example in Table 9.3.

Table 9.3 An example of a text grid

Topic: Acids and their reactions	
Properties	
Class notes	**Library notes**
Turn litmus red Taste sour Have a pH of less than 7 Turns universal indicator red Acid strength is measured by pH.	All acids have hydrogen in them. Alkalis seem to be the opposite of acids. Some gases like sulfur oxides, carbon dioxide, nitrogen oxide dissolve in water making acids. This makes acid rain which attacks carbonate rocks. Hydrogen ion concentration is related to pH.
Reactions	
Class notes	**Library notes**
React with alkalis to make a salt. This is called neutralisation. React with carbonates to produce carbon dioxide.	React with reactive metals to produce hydrogen. Salts are compounds made when hydrogen is replaced by a metal in neutralisation.

PQRS or PQR3

The PQRS or PQR3 approach is a high analytical approach that works well when students read in groups or as a whole class. It is an active reading technique and needs a systematic approach in which all the basic skills of reading are emphasised and developed. The approach comprises the following steps:

1. Students as individuals *preview* the reading by looking at the titles and subtitles, the diagrams in order and the photographs in order. They are asked to decide what they think the passage or section they are about to read is about.
2. Students as a whole class form some *questions* about the passage. These can be very simple, from questions asking about facts to personal questions such as 'What do we expect to find out?' or 'Will the passage tell me about . . . ?' to questions about their skills to read the passage such as 'What do I know already?' and 'Can I skip parts of the reading?'.
3. Students now as individuals *read* the passage with the questions in mind and answer those questions. They should be reminded to reflect on their reading and ask questions such as 'Am I understanding this?'; 'Do I need to read this again?'; 'How do the diagrams and photographs relate to what I have read?'.
4. Students, working in pairs or groups of three, now *reflect and discuss* the questions, the answers and the text and what the text is telling them.
5. Students as individuals now *retell or summarise* what they have read by rewriting in a different genre, or bullet pointing, or producing a quick drawing that illustrates what the text is saying. The following are sought from all students: 'What is the main idea in the text?'; 'How does that relate to my world of experience?'; 'How do I feel about what I have read?'

An example of a text on which this approach could be used is the text on Mercury, Venus and Earth.

Emphasis and bullet pointing

Emphasis and bullet pointing is useful for gifted students since it asks them to read a text, underline, bullet-point list or highlight words, data, phrases or paragraphs that are key concepts and to use different colours in a text to classify ideas that are connected or are opinion or fact, then to link them using arrows. They group those points and retell the piece in their own words. This requires the student to make sense of the work. It is useful for gifted students because it asks them to identify important ideas, link concepts, reorganise text and then to summarise. For example:

> The idea of evolution, an idea of gradual change in living things over long periods of time, is not a new idea. The Greeks put forward a similar idea. Erasmus Darwin, Charles Darwin's grandfather, and the French biologist Lamarck also thought of evolution but they failed to develop the idea to any great extent. Erasmus Darwin did produce an hypothesis that all living things must have had a common microscopic ancestor – a single filament that originated in the sea. Then in 1794 in a book on medicine called *Zoonomia* he recounted on page 496 the idea that 'species can and do change' and further on he refers to the making of 'monstrosities' which we interpret as mutations as animals that have inherited certain wrong characteristics. Charles Darwin, from his work on HMS *Beagle* on its journeys and his collection and careful observation of animals saw that certain animals had a struggle to survive. Those that are successful at surviving pass on qualities to their

Example of text to be analysed by PQRS approach

(Source: Horsfall and O'Brien 2000)

Mercury is the same density as Earth. This heaviness is due to an interior of very heavy metals, possibly iron. Mercury has a diameter of 4878 km and is only 0.38 the size of Earth. This smallness means its mass is only 0.055 that of Earth.

In 1974 and 1975 a spacecraft called *Mariner 10* from Earth passed close by Mercury and photographed it. Like *Mariner 10* I think I will pass this planet by.

Venus

12.13 *Venus*

108.2 million km from the Sun and the next planet, Venus, seems to be different from others. It is revolving in the opposite direction from the others so here the Sun would rise in the west and set in the east. I will need to judge carefully whether I should land on this planet.

Light photons have a favourite way of travelling. We bounce off the surface or atmosphere. You can see Venus from Earth because of the light reflected off the surface. Venus rises in Earth's evening sky and is very bright. Planets can only be seen when they reflect light.

Venus spins very slowly at a very small inclination of 3°. A day here lasts 243 Earth days and a year is 225 Earth days. With a diameter of 12,103 km it is similar in size and density to Earth. Its mass is 0.81 of Earth so its rocks must be different.

Pale yellow clouds of sulphuric acid hide the surface of the planet. These form drops which fall to the surface as acid rain. The atmosphere creates a furnace-like heat because of the carbon dioxide, which traps the Sun's heat like a greenhouse. Temperatures here reach 470°C. Once through the unpleasant atmosphere the surface of Venus is covered with active volcanoes and dry rocks which are so hot that they glow.

This is no place for life. In 1990 *Magellan*, a spacecraft from Earth, succeeded in sending back photos of this corrosive place. A quick bounce off the cloud surface, I think, and I'll pass on to the next planet.

16 Why are the days and years on Mercury different from those on Venus?

17 Draw your idea of the surface of Mercury and Venus.

18 What makes a year on Mercury and Venus shorter than on Earth?

19 How much bigger than Mercury is Venus?

20 What are the things that make Earth so good for life to develop?

Earth

149.6 million km out from the Sun and this planet is another odd one. Earth spins in the same direction as Mercury but is bright blue with white clouds, which constantly shift around the surface.

It spins on its axis at an angle of 23° and takes 1 Earth day (23 hours 56 minutes) to make one full turn. One revolution around the Sun will take it one year (365 days). It has a diameter of 12,756 km and an average temperature of 15°C.

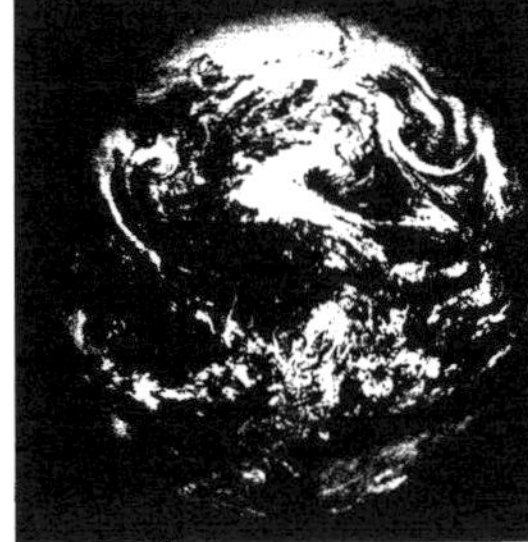

12.14 *Earth*

offspring, which help them to survive. This idea became the 'survival of the fittest'. So in a cold climate the animal that has thick fur that captures the most air between the hairs will survive the extreme conditions. If one of the offspring inherits this characteristic then it will survive in favour of those animals with thin fur.

The student has highlighted ideas they connect with one strand and underlined and highlighted in a different colour those they connect with another theme. Where phrases connect to both they underline and highlight. They now take the component parts and rewrite.

Evolution is gradual change – survival of the fittest. Charles Darwin is identified with the idea of evolution but others before him, Lamarck and Erasmus Darwin, had similar ideas about a common ancestor originating in the sea that evolved into all living things but they failed to develop the idea. Parents pass on characteristics that favour their offspring and offspring pass this on to their offspring and help them survive in the environment, while others die.

CHAPTER 10

What to Look For in the Schemes of Work

The science curriculum for the gifted should integrate process, concepts and content and not separate them into simple structured activities since this will lead to the use of lower level thinking skills.

The objectives to be attained should be explicit in the scheme of work appropriate to the level of expectation to enable a teacher to measure their class against those objectives and set their own expectations as a challenge to the students. The starting place is the expectations box in the QCA National Curriculum schemes of work and the expectations for the higher level students for example:

Expectations box from National Curriculum Scheme of Work for Science Unit 7a Cells (QCA 1999)

At the end of this unit

In terms of scientific enquiry

Most students will: describe some earlier ideas about the structure of living things and relate these to evidence from microscope observations; make observations using a microscope and record them in simple drawings; suggest a question about pollen tubes that can be investigated and use an appropriate sample; present results in an appropriate graph, explaining what these show

Some students will not have made so much progress and will: relate drawings to observations made using a microscope and describe what they found out from their investigation

Some students will have progressed further and will: explain how evidence from microscope observations changed ideas about the structure of living things; estimate sizes of specimens viewed under the microscope and justify the sample chosen in an investigation of pollen tubes

In terms of life processes and living things

Most students will: identify and name features of cells and describe some differences between plant and animal cells; explain that growth occurs when cells divide and increase in size; describe how cells are grouped to form tissues

Some students will not have made so much progress and will: recognise that all organisms are made from cells and name some parts of a cell

Some students will have progressed further and will: recognise that viruses are not cells and describe how some cells in an organism are specialised to carry out particular functions

In this example the level of thinking is highlighted and the higher level students will be expected to engage in activities that cover the range shown in Table 10.1.

Table 10.1 Analysis of the range of activities expected in Module 7A Cells

Science attainment target	Expectation	Thinking skills are
1	Explain, estimate, justify	Comprehend, analysis evaluation
2	Recognise, describe specialisation related to function	Know, comprehend, analysis evaluation
Concept range	Cells parts Classification Animal cells, plant cells bacteria, viruses Organelles Micro-processes Macro-processes Tissues	

Therefore to match these expectations the types of activity in the curriculum will relate to the higher order skills and focus upon:

- developing higher order thinking skills using **conceptual language**;
- directed activities relating to **text** for **developing higher order** study **skills**;
- in-depth study topics that **emphasise** a **'real product'** outcome.

This analytical approach to differentiating the teaching of science requires careful planning by the identification of differentiated **learning objectives**. To enable the student to become part of the assessment process these learning objectives need to be converted into **behavioural learning objectives** by using adjectives that describe a **learning outcome** that could be combined into targets using the sort of language shown in the lists below.

Knowledge *Observations and recall of information*	**Comprehension** *Describe what you mean*	**Application** *Use knowledge and information in different contexts*
Remember Recognise Repeat/recall Find Know Identify Copy Describe Observe Recite Memorise Tell Fill in missing information Recite or write down	Explain Provide example Translate Interpret facts Reason Summarise Infer Compare Solve Understand Précis Order and predict Restate	Select Solve Use other information, prior knowledge, methods, or concepts to: Build Communicate Construct Describe Measure Create Experiment/make/trial Present Prioritise Solve problems

	Creative thinking	Critical thinking
Analysis *Organising and recognising components which apply to learning*	**Synthesis** *Relate knowledge and understanding from a number of areas*	**Evaluation** *Can make judgements based on intervention*
Sort Explore Classify Categorise Sequence Compare/contrast Cause/consequence Bias Problem solve Hypothesise Be critical Question Review See patterns Estimate	Create Construct Combine Hypothesise/predict Invent Correlate Think up solutions Transfer understanding Negotiate Form theories Enquiry Problem solving Complex thinking Investigate Compose	Assess Appraise Justify Review Prioritise Grade Recommend Estimate Decision making Reasoning Draw conclusions Compare/discriminate Judge Research Verify Recognise subjectivity Make objective choices

The objectives and outcomes can be obtained from the scheme of work or from a list such as above but they need working into the scheme of work to enable teachers teaching out of discipline to link them to the differing abilities being considered. One department's approach is shown below (**bold** = gifted range).

Example: Year 7 – Identification of progression of learning objectives

Previous experience from Key Stage 2 schemes of work and school information

- Mixing materials, e.g. adding salt to water, can cause them to change.
- Some changes can be reversed and some cannot.
- Some solids dissolve in water to give a solution, e.g. salt and sugar; some substances, e.g. chalk and sand, do not dissolve in water.
- Some solids dissolve more easily when the water is hot.
- There is a limit to the amount of solid that can be dissolved in water.
- Dissolved materials can be recovered by evaporation and crystallising.

Objectives to be developed in Key Stage 3 Year 7 classes

- Solutes dissolve in different amounts of solvent at different temperatures.
- Solutes dissolve in different amounts in different solvents at the same temperature.
- When physical changes take place, e.g. formation of solutions, then mass is conserved.
- Explain dissolving using the particulate theory.

- **Graphically represent solubility at different temperatures for given solutes and solvents.**
- **Interpret the graph and explain differing rates of solubility using models.**

Keywords

Solid	Liquid	Salt	Compound	Dissolve
Mixture	Change	Reversible	Solute	Solvent
Solution	Particle	Space	**Temperature**	**Energy**
Volume	**Mass**			

Misconceptions that could be held by pupils in Year 7

- A tendency to concentrate on the solute only. They decide the solute has disappeared because it cannot be seen. They sometimes use the word melted to describe disappeared.
- They can regard the solvent as a continuous medium and will understand the solid forming particles. The solvent will then flow in between the particles. If challenged they will also state air fills the spaces between particles.
- Some will consider the solution as a continuous medium and the solid has melted into water.
- Filtering reinforces the misconception of a continuous medium and they will talk of molecules of salt or sugar but rarely of water molecules.
- Confusion over mass, weight and volume.
- When things dissolve they disappear and they will weigh nothing.
- Molecules are solid bits and they stick together.

The identification of learning objectives and possible misconceptions lead to the following progression of learning outcomes for Year 7:

Progression of the concept of dissolving

- Some solids, like salt and sugar, dissolve in water.
- When something dissolves it is soluble.
- When a substance is soluble it is called a solute.
- The liquid that dissolves the solute is called a solvent.
- When a solute dissolves in a solvent a solution is formed.
- Some solids like chalk and sand do not dissolve in water. They are insoluble.
- **Particles in insoluble substances can be very big or clumped together.**

Progression of the concept of solubility

- Some chemicals, e.g. copper sulphate and sodium carbonate, dissolve in water.
- Some chemicals, e.g. calcium carbonate and copper oxide, do not dissolve in water.
- Not all solutes dissolve to the same extent in the same amount of water.
- Hot liquids dissolve more solute than cold liquids.
- Gases can dissolve in water. *Bridging concept* – fish gills, temperature/oxygen.

- When no more solute will dissolve in a solvent the solution is called a saturated solution.
- **A graph can be drawn of mass of solute dissolved against temperature or volume of solvent.**
- **Differing rates of solubility for different salts in water can be explained by the size of particles and differing attractive forces.**

Progression of the concept of crystallisation

- Dissolving is temporary and so is a physical change.
- The solute can be recovered by evaporation of the solvent.
- Solutes crystallise by cooling. This can be observed under a microscope.
- **Cooling a solution at different temperature rates changes the size of crystals.** ***Bridging concept*** **– Relate differing sizes of particles to rocks such as granite, basalt and obsidian and mineral particle size.**

Progression of a particulate model explanation of dissolving

- In a solid the particles are held in a rigid shape and gently vibrate.
- In a liquid the particles roll over each other and are loosely held.
- Solids, liquids and gases have mass and volume and so must take up space.
- When solutes dissolve the mass will change in relation to the combined mass but the volume will not generally be a combination of the volumes of both solute and solvent.
- Particles of a liquid move between the particles of a solid and separate them so they spread out between the particles of the liquid.
- **When a liquid is heated energy is transferred and the movement of the particles is faster and the kinetic energy contributes to the breaking up of a solute by a solvent.**
- **Differing attractive forces between particles in solids and solvent particles can explain differing rates and amounts of dissolving.** ***Bridging concept*** **– reactions in solution are easier than in solid state.**

This progression of learning objectives leads to differing routes through the Year 7 topic on dissolving things, as shown in Figure 10.1.

After identification of the progression of objectives and outcomes the teacher needs to identify the most appropriate learning styles, type of activity or strategy to help the differing groups of students learn and achieve the objectives. Next the teacher should identify the roles, language demand, and audience for the product that would vary the level of differentiation.

Hughes (1997) has attempted to give a summary of the effectiveness of some teaching strategies used by teachers. He identifies the active processes of research, practical or active work, class or group discussions, role play, video and ICT simulations and modelling, high interactive demonstrations, individual interview and help and active reading as being the most effective and reliable for developing high levels of learning.

When much science work is examined it is often found to be without direct relevance to everyday society, formulaic, one of following recipes for practical work and reading and recording paradigms of knowledge without personal interaction.

Common introduction to the topic

- Some solids like salt and sugar dissolve in water.
- When something dissolves it is soluble.
- When a substance is soluble it is called a solute.
- The liquid that dissolves the solute is called a solvent.
- When a solute dissolves in a solvent a solution is formed.
- Some solids like chalk and sand do not dissolve in water.

From this common starting point there are two routes possible. The least able and average generally take Route A and the more able take Route B.

Route A: least able and average ability

- Solids, liquids and gases have mass and volume.
- Dissolving is a temporary change.
- Some chemicals like copper sulphate and sodium carbonate dissolve in water.
- Some chemicals like calcium carbonate and copper oxide do not dissolve in water.
- Not all solutes dissolve to the same amount in water.
- The solute can be recovered by evaporation.
- A solute can be crystallised by cooling. This can be observed under a microscope.
- **Cooling a solution at different rates changes the size of the crystals.**
- **Bridging concept – Relate differing sizes of particles to rocks such as granite, basalt and obsidian.**

Route B: more able pupils

- Some chemicals like copper sulphate and sodium carbonate dissolve in water.
- Some chemicals like calcium carbonate and copper oxide do not dissolve in water.
- Not all solutes dissolve to the same extent in the same amount of water.
- Cooling a solution at different rates changes the size of the crystals.
- Hot liquids dissolve more solute than cold liquids.
- Gases can dissolve in water. Bridging concept – fish gills, temperature and oxygen.
- When no more solute will dissolve in a solvent the solution is called a saturated solution.
- **A graph can be drawn of mass of solute dissolved against temperature or volume of solvent.**
- **Differing rates of solubility for different salts in water can be explained by size of particles and differing attractive forces.**

Both routes need to use the particulate model to help develop an explanation for dissolving and solubility so the lighter text needs to be built into the work for all.

Consolidation for topic (bold only for able science pupils)

- Matter is composed of particles.
- In a solid the particles are held in a rigid shape and gently vibrate.
- In a liquid the particles roll over each other and are loosely held.
- Particles of a liquid move between the particles of a solid and separate them so they spread out between the particles of the liquid.
- **When a liquid is heated energy is transferred to the particles and the movement of the particles is faster and this kinetic energy contributes to the breaking up of a solute by a solvent.**
- **Differing attractive forces between particles in a solid and between solvent particles and solute particles can explain differing rates and amounts of dissolving.**
- **Reactions in solution are easier and faster than reactions in solids.**

Leads to an end of module test – summative assessment

Figure 10.1 Differing routes through the Year 7 topic on dissolving things

This means the cognitive aspects of conceptual understanding are being outpaced by the need to follow and understand the basic facts to 'jump hurdles' or pass prescribed tests. For the gifted science student's learning to be effective the cognitive aspects need to be engaged. An activity that would meet these outcomes could look like the following.

Example of engaging the cognitive aspects of learning

Investigating cells by team research and discussion – language and cooperative group work

Aims

- To help students learn about the cell and the relationship of parts of the cell.
- To explain the relationship of micro-processes to macro-processes in tissues in an organ such as the liver.
- To develop illustrative language to help build word models.
- To develop the team-working skills of the gifted student.
- To listen and debate other points of view and prioritise an argument.

Outcomes

- To describe the parts of a cell and their function in the cell.
- To explain how parts of a cell relate to each other and the importance of that part to the working of the cell.
- To state and demonstrate how cells specialise to form a tissue and explain how that relates to the various jobs of tissues in an organ like the liver.
- To use scientifically accurate but imaginative language to write a script about a scientific system such as the cell.

Organisation

Prior work:
Students have worked in mixed ability groups to learn about the cell, part by teacher input and part by group research using textbooks. They have drawn generalised diagrams of cells and seen a short video about cell structure. They have been involved in a whole-class simulation and an ICT simulation about the cell and how it works.

The students have been grouped by ability and the gifted group have been given the role of programme researchers researching and drafting a script for a youth radio programme on the cells of the liver and liver disease due to excessive drinking. As individuals they work for 10 minutes on targeted research on cell parts and their purpose, for example cell membrane, nucleus, cytoplasm and mitochondria.

Back in their groups they work for 20 minutes and must decide how the cell might carry out the jobs identified in the article used as source research material: 'Libby the liver cell – The Body's Chemical Factory' in *Science Web Reader – Biology* (O'Brien 2000). They also have access to free material from the health service and chemists on drinking and liver disease.

The material must be scripted for a radio programme and can be recorded by tape recording to occupy no more than 5 minutes on a tape. They can elect to produce a cartoon, an A1 poster or folded A4 handout.

Assessment

The script, any presentation and any tape they produce should be organised and carefully discuss the important points. It should be linked and be logical with reference to science ideas. The script should use accurate science language but explain carefully, in everyday language, any scientific or technical words. It must be exciting to help people understand the theme without the use of diagrams.

Metacognitive reflection

1. How well did you work as a team?
2. Did you organise the research and agree about the facts?
3. Which activity did you enjoy the most and which gave you the most challenge?
4. How does this work on the cell help you understand the relationship of cells to tissues and organs?

CHAPTER 11

Using Science Attainment Target 1 (Sc1)

A common sense definition of science could be 'proven knowledge'; an activity in which science theories are derived from experience by experiment and observation, creating a wholly objective view of science, one in which inductive argument could be seen as the main tool to determine scientific fact, taking many experiences and generalising the observations to maintain objectivity. It is legitimised by repeated observations under different conditions with the use of a deductive argument in which predictions and explanations provide the logic.

The nature of science is one area that can be used to create differentiation in the science curriculum for gifted students. Many gifted students in science illustrate some of the characteristics of good scientists and it is their perception that poses them problems leading to the view that school science is too structured.

Einstein described scientists as people 'with a passion to explain' and certainly scientists do have a desire to explain. An examination of the way they attempt to explain science reveals a difference in the practice of professional science and in the teaching of science in school.

The main method used by the professional scientist to develop understanding in science is to develop models. The Association for Science Education (ASE) working party (1994) identified science models as representations of a novel object, event or idea of scientific interest in terms of a more familiar object, event or idea. The notion is that these models are tested to the point they no longer work and then are readjusted to create more appropriate models. In this way models evolve to suit different purposes and gifted students will be aware of analogies they use to describe science processes.

In school science the approach is an inductive one, concerned with the development of general laws and paradigms in which the student is frequently expected to repeat a learned model. For the gifted science student, who wishes to experiment with learned models in greater detail, with their own ideas and, like the scientist in the field, develop their own personal model from the conventional model, this can be unsatisfying. The short structured packaged science lessons often do not allow the gifted science student the opportunity to 'fly on their own'. There is often not the time for the reflective style of learning which leads to creativity.

Robin Millar (1989) defines science education as one using the inductive approach to develop an intellectual viewpoint and describes the process as one: 'of passing on knowledge and understanding of science and its practices to new learners'. This inductive view of science can create a very mechanical approach to the teaching, in which the student looks for the 'right answer' and loses the excitement of looking for the most probable solution.

Unfortunately a good deal of secondary school science teaching has taken on a reactive aspect, in which creativity is limited by the dominance of the inductive teaching approach. The inductive argument approach is very appealing in its simplicity and desire to attribute substantive proof to allow one to give an adequate explanation and is the basis of science education in the early years, primary and much of the secondary science of the average and below average student.

However creativity is the very essence, the joy, of doing science. Sc1 is perceived to be an area that should present opportunities for science creativity. However the nature of school Sc1 often does not fully address creativity because of its reliance upon developing expertise in the process-skills and techniques of science, by structured approaches intended to link procedural understanding to conceptual understanding. In this atmosphere extension takes on the form of extending the procedures relating to measurement, validity and reliability and not always the relationships between concepts.

A student's experience of doing science as a cultural pursuit develops their image of the science and helps to crystallise their opinion and perspectives of the discipline of science and its relevance to them as individuals. The gifted are very much aware of the culture of the subject and they feed more off the enthusiasm and excitement of the teacher than off the knowledge. It is interesting to note that in surveys of professional scientists 95 per cent of them state that they came into science because of the enthusiasm and excitement generated by one of more of their teachers. Exploration and questioning the nature of science should be present in science education. Its function is to help students develop the ability to form and use models as a tool for explanation and to expect to get them wrong and learn from trying to make them work.

Richard Feynman, the Nobel physicist who found his science education wanting, described his way of exploring as visualisation of a vague indefinable thing in which he saw equations as coloured letters mixed with symbols (Gribbin and Gribbin 1997). However, it must be stated students cannot work in a vacuum – *Ex nihilo nihil fit* – or as Charlie Mingus the jazz musician expressed it: 'You can't improvise from nothing, you have to improvise from something.' There is a requirement for good science teaching but teaching that is sensitive to the needs of the student and their learning.

Any teaching must impart knowledge but leave time and opportunity for students to be creative with ideas. It must provide the gifted students with the tools to think. If exploration is seen as a time for observing, then creativity should be seen as freethinking the opportunity to play with ideas to solve a problem. An interesting example of this is that when watching a student playing frisbee with a patterned plate, Feynman noted the spinning of the pattern to be faster than the wobble of the plate. From his observations he went on to work out the equations of wobbles and some time later realised this seemingly play activity could be applied to electron orbits and it was from these diagrams and equations he was awarded the Nobel Prize.

The construction of a concept model is an important step towards the internalisation of an idea. It will not be a perfect model but one that develops with more experience. There is much evidence from Ros Driver *et al.* (1994) and others on the way students play with imperfect models to explain events and slowly construct concepts. This approach to the teaching of science does engender some of the flavour of a paradigm approach to the learning of science because it calls for the experiences of the student to be shared, accounted and challenged by teachers and others.

The design of a curriculum for the gifted students, to allow them the opportunity to develop time for creative thinking and learn to appreciate differing views of science, must be one of the first things for heads of departments to consider with their team.

In Attainment Target 1 there is the link between creative and critical thinking. The process of thinking and problem solving in science can be viewed as shown in Figure 11.1.

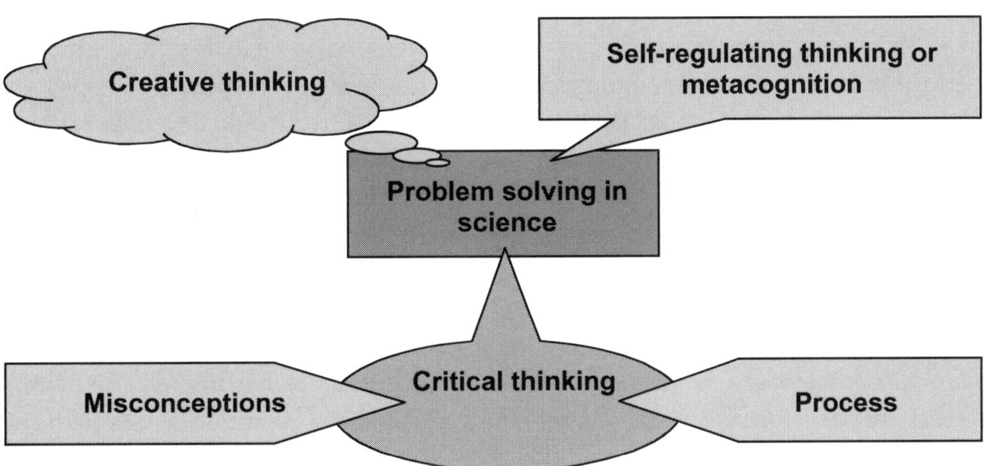

Figure 11.1 The process of thinking and problem solving

Creative thinking is concerned with engagement in activities where an answer is not apparent or easily seen and is characterised by the student engaging in:

- thinking laterally and engaging in thought experiments to test ideas and make predictions;
- having the ability to analysis information and data for relevance;
- synthesising and recreating material to fit the situation and make it appropriate for the context;
- evaluating and pushing their thinking and knowledge into areas they may not have been to before.

Critical thinking is a reflective process in which the student:

- demonstrates an open-mindedness and thinks with clarity and accuracy;
- displays the ability to listen and reason leading to the ability to debate a position of thought with sensitivity to alternative viewpoints.

Critical thinking skills relate to:

- observing and inferring;
- comparing and contrasting;
- recognising cause and effect;

- defining operations and methods;
- developing models to explain.

The relationship between conceptual and procedural understanding is a useful tool for differentiation for the most able and the involvement of mathematical analysis can further differentiate, particularly if this is a joint initiative with the mathematics department. The design of an activity involving exploration or investigation must consider the type of practical and level of demand with the depth of idea and model. With an understanding of the process and concepts involved it is possible to differentiate an investigation.

Differentiation of an investigation requires an active decision in the planning to make either the conceptual or procedural understanding demand aspect high or, with the exceptionally able, both areas equally high. When the procedural skill is important then the conceptual understanding should be low and the emphasis on questions related to the procedural skills. Differentiation for the gifted would be concerned with degrees of precision, accuracy, reliability and validity of results and the application of the concept to interpret the evidence and data relevant to the conclusion.

When the emphasis is on concept acquisition and consolidation the design of the activity should emphasise the relationship between interacting concepts and models while lowering the procedural skills and demand. Differentiation could be related to a consideration of data analysis by looking for and identifying inter-relationships and correlations between multivariate data to support conclusions. This would necessitate the formation of models and generalised theories to explain the phenomena. An example of altering the balance between procedural and conceptual understanding is shown in Table 11.1.

Table 11.1 Example of altering the balance between procedural and conceptual understanding

	Emphasis placed on level of each			
Procedural understanding	**Low**	**High**	**Low**	**High**
Conceptual understanding	**Low**	**Low**	**High**	**High**
Rate of reaction	Does the chemical dissolve in water? (Observation)	What affects the rate of dissolving? (Measurement)	What affects the hardness of water? (Observation)	What affects the rate of reaction of sodium thiosulphate + acid? (Measurement)
	Does the chemical dissolve faster in hot or cold water?	Is it size of bits? Is it the temperature? Is it the stirring?	How does the presence of some salts affect the lathering of soap? Is there a general relationship?	Is the relationship linear? If not why? What does that mean?

Investigations can be differentiated by:

- changing the degree of openness by controls;
- consideration of the number of, range and nature of the variables;

- consideration of the nature of interaction of variables and the way they will change;
- considering the range of accuracy and precision;
- the nature of the pattern of relationship in the results;
- the level of evaluation in relation to reliability and validity.

The important thing to bear in mind is that for these forms of differentiation to be effective there has to be a balance between active and focused teaching on the concepts of evidence and creative thought in order for the students to develop a confidence and improve their reasoning ability.

Example of extension by procedural and conceptual understanding

Plant nutrients

Source: adapted from *Bedfordshire Activities for Process Science* (BAPS) Pack 2 'Plant Trouble' (Bedfordshire Education Service 1988)

Outcomes

- To use research skills information to find out about plant nutrients.
- To design an experiment with control of variables and discussion of the difficulty of controlling variables in plant investigations.
- To determine some method of measuring the differences observed.
- To determine how they will present those results and analyse them to form a conclusion that considers the process by which plants obtain their nutrients.

The task

A farmer has a problem with his barley. The plants are looking weak and slightly yellow. He is well aware that plants need certain elements or nutrients to help them grow. His problem is he does not know what elements plants need or which ones are missing from his field. As plant scientists working on plant growth, he has passed the problem to you to solve. You are to write a report for him explaining the reasons for your conclusion. Most important in the report is to indicate the variables, control and how your results helped you get to that conclusion.

Organisation

Prior work:
A topic on plant growth and photosynthesis in which students show good understanding of the differences between photosynthesis and respiration. They are aware of the roots and plant transport systems.

To extend this topic this exercise makes them consider the various needs of plants to help them grow. The intention is to set up an experiment to investigate the effects of different nutrients. They work in small groups of three and investigate the farmer's problem. Their aim is to produce a report in plain English for the farmer using accurate science and with a glossary of specific words they use.

Assessment

The report they produce should be organised and carefully illustrate the important ideas they have come up with about the effect of different elements on plant growth. It should indicate an overview of procedure with clear and accurate discussion of the variables and the controls they set up. An important consideration is the way they determine to measure the differences and form conclusions. As a report it should be concise, clear, in good English and organised. They should use accurate science language but explain any science or technical words in an appendix glossary. It should be scientifically correct. It must be an easy read with clear diagrams to help people understand the theme.

Evaluation

The students find the task challenging and the design of the experiment with controls can cause some students difficulty. They can encounter difficulties in determining what should be measured. A few will decide plant height is a good indicator while others decide leaf colour is a good indicator. The colour idea is a difficult one to measure but could be done using an ICT solution.

Other topics for Sc1 enquiry could be:

- People like to dunk biscuits and recent research has shown that dunking biscuits into a milky drink enhances the flavour since the fat forms around the food flavours and locks it in. This dunking weakens the biscuit because it either melts the fat which holds the biscuit together or dissolves the sugars holding the biscuit together. What would be useful to know would be is there any relationship linking the 'dunkability' of different biscuits to temperature of drink and amount of milk and the type of biscuit? Design an experiment to determine the 'dunkability coefficient' of different biscuits.
- Put four tablespoons of sugar and two tablespoons of golden syrup or honey in a saucepan. Bring to the boil and simmer gently for five minutes stirring from time to time. Add a heaped teaspoon of baking soda and stir quickly. What happens? Why does that happen? What will happen to the substance as it cools? What does this tell us about rock formation?
- Investigate the growth of young cress cells to determine where the most growth takes place and how that growth takes place.
- Using data analysis make a list of problems facing horticulturalists and arable farmers in Britain. Classify them into groups such as problems due to climate, disease, terrain.
- Investigate how particle size affects visibility through water and develop a calibration graph using milk as the dispersant. Then investigate the settling of sediments and try to determine how flowing muddy water produces different forms of sediments.
- Investigate the combustion properties and compounds of sulfur and magnesium. Predict and justify if selenium and calcium would be similar.
- Investigate why there is a limiting length for a drinking straw.
- Investigate how changes in heat affect elastic bands. Try to develop a model to explain the phenomenon.

Sources of Sc1 investigations

Davies, K. (1990) *In Search of Solutions.* London: Royal Society of Chemistry.

Farley, R. (2001) *School Chemistry Experiments.* Hatfield: Association for Science Education.

Gibbs, K. (1999) *The Resourceful Physics Teacher*. London: Institute of Physics.

Horsfall, P. (2000) *Science Web Enquiry Pack 1* and *Pack 2*. Cheltenham: Nelson Thornes.

Salters: The Chemistry Club Handbook 1 and 2. London: The Salters Company.

Taylor, J. (1995) *In Search of More Solutions*. London: Royal Society of Chemistry.

Warren, D. (2001) *Chemists in a Social and Historical Context*. London: Royal Society of Chemistry.

Sang, D. and Wood-Robinson, V. (eds) (2002) *Teaching Secondary Scientific Enquiry*. London: John Murray.

CHAPTER 12

Extension by Use of Models and Generalised Theories

All students require focused teaching at the right level to support their learning, develop the concepts and ideas of science and help them form mental models to enable them to understand the science. The danger is this can be too structured and focus too much on developing a bed or paradigm of factual knowledge. In all students we must try to develop a sense of wonder, a feeling of awe when they see something new, but the joy for the gifted student comes in the attempt to explain for themselves what lies behind the event. As I. Pavlov stated: 'Do not become a mere recorder of facts, but try to penetrate the mystery of their origin.'

In science a model is a postulated structure for an object or event that makes use of the notions of analogy and metaphor (ASE 1994). Their strength is in helping us to penetrate the mystery, to offer explanations where wonder might persist. A most colourful and useful example of a model is the 'map' of the London Underground. It is not a map since it does not represent distance nor true pathways of the tracks, but it does present to us a picture that helps us to comprehend where stations are and how we can travel across London without the need of a compass. It is elegant in its simplicity and informative in its structure. Scientific models can be of the same elegance.

Models are one of the most powerful tools for identifying the strong misconceptions held by students. Students can often answer direct questions with correct answers but when applying ideas the model they use displays their true deep understanding of the system.

Our skills as teachers lie in recognising a student's misconceptions and challenging them in such a way that they change their views to a model that works in all situations. As teachers we need to appreciate in our students the notion of the continuous development of ideas by a student's continuous re-examination of their own misconceptions. Students move from one inaccurate model to another until they have one that works.

By presenting ideas to gifted students in a form that allows them to finish off or reflect on ideas and reconstruct understanding for themselves and by not presenting knowledge in a finished form, teachers give them the opportunity to develop their own models. There are research materials from a large number of researchers, both in Europe and worldwide, which indicate a number of strong misconceptions held by students in their thinking about science. Teachers looking for a more central collection of this area of misconceptions in children's science will find the material collected by Driver *et al.* (1994) worthwhile support material. Through classroom evaluations misconceptions have been identified as being of great significance in all students by causing conceptual blocks in problem solving and in the later development of science ideas.

There is an apocryphal story, whose origin is obscure, about a group of gifted physics doctorate students who were set three problems, dealing with attempts to move objects. They were asked to solve:

- Problem 1: Move a large boulder that has rolled onto a wet lawn and become lodged in the turf.
- Problem 2: Move a broken down car on an inclined motorway.
- Problem 3: Move a particle in a particle accelerator.

When all their solutions were recorded and all their jottings collected and examined it revealed they used three different models to solve the problems. For the stone problem the model was Aristotelian, for the car they used a Newtonian model and for the particle a quantum model was used. Yet they solved all three problems adequately. It does illustrate our mental models and misconceptions can be influenced by the context of the learning and that declaring one model wrong and another right could be an academic exercise if the student produces the correct answer. The important characteristic of the gifted is that they realise the limitations of a model and will attempt to solve the problem with another model.

Hence when dealing with gifted students it is important to realise they can frequently use faulty logic to solve a problem. Faulty logic is when the student appears to be using a misconception but, behind their model, the student is holding on to an idea that will rectify the end result, as in the above examples. Close open-ended questioning can reveal the student has an acceptable scientific paradigm.

Faulty logic is the result of a student's reconstructing models or processes to develop a personal method to solve a problem. It is common in mathematical situations and mathematics teachers will often comment on the novel ways students develop to solve problems. This fuzziness in using models or processes to solve problems is a metacognitive strategy used to bridge a gap in understanding and displays, in the student, a high degree of thinking about the problem and their own limitations in solving it.

Our skill as teachers has to be in identifying those real gaps in understanding and bridging them or providing the students with the tools to do it themselves. A common mistake is to criticise the student's approach and teach a complete model to the student without attacking the actual problem. To the gifted student this causes frustration and the student may just give up if this approach is used too frequently. By examining and discussing their models we can help students diagnose their weak areas and suggest alternative strategies. One powerful tool here is the use of concept cartoons such as those developed by Keogh and Naylor (1999).

So in teaching science concepts to the gifted there must be many opportunities for them to become more aware of their own mental models and they should make use of their models to solve problems. They should also try to develop models for themselves to allow them to demonstrate creativity in their thinking. One simple exercise is to try to explain what happens to the molecules in a rubber ball when it bounces.

Extension work in the biological sciences

Areas within the biological sciences that present themselves as good choices for progression with the gifted student using models are to:

- explain the structure and function of life processes from micro to macro;
- explain the maintenance of the internal environment of plants or animals;
- describe processes in animals and cells using both mechanical and abstract models;
- explain the transfer of genetic characteristics either by using 3D structures such as popper beads or by the use of ICT;
- describe classification as more than a process of grouping organisms but more as a concept of similarities and differences linked to genetic transfer;
- use ICT or flow charts to model the transfer of energy in a living system using simulations of food chains and webs;
- use ICT to model the inter-relationship between organisms, including decomposition and the recycling of constituent elements and compounds;
- develop the structure of an organ by discussing the needs of an organism such as the structure of leaves on a plant adapted to hot dry conditions;
- describe the possible ways a function could be carried out and the limitations imposed by the conditions under which the organism lives such as when disease strikes or the environment changes;
- describe cross-curricular issues such as the human impact on the equilibrium of populations and pollution by various agents from industry. These can be modelled using ICT, role play or simulations.

In biology there is evidence of gifted students not being fully confident in their modelling of the processes of life in the cell and in organs. They can lack rigour in their scientific consideration of the life processes because they frequently view them in a fragmentary way with little concern for the relationship between the organisation of cells and the structure of a tissue leading to an organ. Specifically they know the processes of photosynthesis and respiration but do not understand the relationship between the two in plants.

The concept of classification is a difficult area in which students can show a weakness in understanding the relationships between organisms in the same group and in developing a feel for the genetic basis of classification, such as a concept of species. They demonstrate some confusion over the process of growth as increase in cell number and the transfer of genetic material from cell to cell and some see genetic transfer as synonymous with reproduction. The relationship of bacteria to the cycle of materials is not fully appreciated and they frequently consider decomposition as separate from other living processes, viewing it almost entirely as a chemical process.

Extension work in chemistry

In chemistry the following areas present themselves as good areas for developing extension work using abstract models developed from mathematics or ICT:

- the particulate theory to explain the idea of collisions between particles accounting for reactions and the patterns of properties linked to structural factors;

- bonding and structure using electrons and the idea of charge differences in some molecules assisted by software;
- introducing the concept of equilibrium in chemical reactions using simple systems and qualitative considerations leading to a model using ICT;
- the idea of representing equations by symbols and further development of the mole concept;
- the use of equations to represent electro-chemical reactions developed with the use of spreadsheets in ICT, use of simulations or jigsaw puzzle style exercises;
- developing models of energy transfer in reactions using the concept of bond energy – again this can be developed using ICT with spreadsheets, or problem-solving exercises;
- environmental effects of certain chemicals and looking for a balance;
- the rock cycle and plate tectonics with consideration of the geochemical processes.

In chemistry most misconceptions relate to students' understanding of the particulate model, the conservation of matter and mass, and the transfer of energy.

Particulate concepts are often complicated with a confused view of a continuous and discontinuous model of matter, so some students view the space between atoms as being filled with something, often air. The relation of physical change as a change in the organisation of particles and chemical change as a change in the combination of particles is not fully appreciated, so they are comfortable with the macro-expression of a chemical reaction or a change in state, but their particulate models are imperfect, hence they find equation work difficult. This can be helped by using balls to represent the bits in a chemical reaction and changing them around to represent reactions.

The concept of energy in chemical and physical change is often confused. Rises in temperature are sometimes regarded as products of the reaction and they have difficulty in appreciating the difference between heat and temperature. They view chemical reactions as isolated systems and often the student does not consider the origin of the energy transferred in a chemical reaction.

Extension work in physics

In physics, extension can be developed using the concept of energy transfer. It is important to develop a working model of what energy transfer is, and to be able to mathematically model the transfer of energy. Other areas of extension are the following:

- a knowledge of the difference between temperature and heat;
- develop the concept of internal heat;
- develop the idea of charge flow, current and voltage with a mathematical model;
- represent the behaviour of electrical devices using mathematical models and ICT simulations;
- using mathematical and theoretical models to explain electromagnetism;
- investigate the motion of objects, especially in curved trajectories such as satellites, assisted by using software;

- wave characteristics using mathematics to model frequency, wave length and resonance;
- using Russell Stannard's *Uncle Albert and the Quantum Quest* (1994) for discussion and presentations to introduce students to the ideas of quantum physics;
- origins of the universe and particles using books such as *Black Holes* Couper and Henbest (1996).

The concept of energy is difficult to develop because of the cultural differences between the way physicists, chemists and biologists model energy transfers. However, it is important for the student to develop a working model of energy transfer. This is important in the consideration of the differences between temperature and heat and the idea of particle movement and kinetic energy. The use of terms like energy stores develops a particular view of energy leading to some misconception but it is important to develop a language that, while being descriptive, does not lead to imprecision in the model.

The view of electrical current flow as a sequential process coupled with the concept of the battery as a store of electrons develops early in students and is a difficult one to shift but it does cause problems when considering the relationship between current and voltage. This is an area that needs frequent exploration and expansion to develop the conceptual model of the student. Care needs to be taken when using mathematics since it can obscure the manipulative model the student uses to explain systems.

Using ICT to model and predict the behaviour of different systems using spreadsheets or simulations is still not fully exploited by teachers, particularly when working with the gifted. It is important to get home the idea that we can analyse graphs using mathematics such as the use of $y = mx + c$ and the use of curves on graphs are ways of considering what is happening. It is important to develop in students the transfer of mathematical skills to help them manipulate formulae once they have learnt to mathematically model a system.

Example of enrichment by modelling using spreadsheets

Variation arising from genetic and environment factors

Source: Understanding Biology through Problem Solving (Hoey 1991)

Outcomes

- To state how genes and the environment cause organisms to have differences and justify with examples.
- To analyse the changes in population represented as a histogram.
- To demonstrate how spreadsheets can be used to model ideas by comparing the shapes of two charts.
- To explain why there were differences in two different samples of fish and distinguish between genetic and environmental differences.

The task

You are a geneticist exploring the problem of variation (differences between individuals in a population) arising from environmental and genetic factors. You know differences between individuals brought about by genetic factors are often difficult to isolate from differences brought about by environmental factors. To get some idea of the genetic differences all the organisms have to reproduce and be developed under exactly the same controlled environmental conditions. This is difficult to achieve for large organisms but with small organisms being farmed it is possible to get very close to those conditions. You have access to the following data from a trout fish farm in the south of England.

Trout hatcheries control the environment very carefully and any variations between individuals will be mainly due to genetic differences. The table shows the size of young trout in 1987 and 1988.

Length (cm)	No. in length interval	
	in 1987	in 1988
7.5–7.9	0	2
8.0–8.4	9	5
8.5–8.9	16	8
9.0–9.4	51	17
9.5–9.9	105	40
10.0–10.4	115	50
10.5–10.9	84	54
11.0–11.4	41	34
11.5–11.9	49	20
12.0–12.4	16	8
12.5–12.9	10	6
13.0–13.4	4	4
13.5–13.9	0	2

- Explain why the differences will be genetic and not environmental and why that is important for this work and for genetic engineering.
- Enter data into a spreadsheet and convert to percentages of trout in each length interval for each year.
- Construct histograms to show the variation in length of trout within each sample population.
- Which year has the widest range in trout length?
- What percentage of trout in each year has a length of more than 11.9 cm?
- Expressed as a ratio, what is the difference in the number present in the length intervals 8.5–8.9 cm as seen in the two years?
- Apart from environmental differences, what factor in the procedure makes any comparison between the samples unreliable?
- Describe two factors that should be kept constant in the environment if a fair comparison of variation in lengths is to be made between the two samples.

As a geneticist supporting genetic manipulation prepare an article for a farming magazine about genetic variation and how it can affect an organism. Describe the factors that may change to create variation. Decide if there is a relationship controlling the size of fish to be used for food. What could be controlling the size of young fish over the period of time before fish are large enough for eating? Describe how the hatcheries might change conditions to keep some consistency about the size of the fish they produce.

Organisation

This exercise attempts to link the idea of genetic variation and farming practice to indicate that farming is a controlled genetic manipulation. It is expected the students will look at a range of factors. Overall it is important they use ICT to develop a model for comparing populations from a graphical representation. Using a crib they enter a formula in the spreadsheet for calculating percentages.

Metacognitive reflection

- How well did you work on your own?
- Did you research and reflect on the meaning of the information?
- Which activity did you enjoy the most and which gave you the most challenge?
- How does this work help you understand genetic manipulation and has it helped you form a view?

Assessment

The report has to be organised carefully and illustrated with diagrams to help people understand the idea of genetic variation and to display the important points about it. It has to use accurate language, providing explanations of any science or technical words, and be scientifically correct. It has to show the use of a model to determine a course of action for the farmer. The modelling involves use of a formula to calculate percentage and students have to compare the charts. Answers to the questions have to be part of the main text.

Evaluation

The students find the task challenging. The use of a computer spreadsheet is less of a difficulty for the majority but a few still struggle with the manipulation of formulae. Using the information to draw a graph proves a very easy task and they should all interpret the changes in the curve and attempt to offer some possible factors that could affect the variation and factors to be controlled.

Summary

Develop models and ideas by concentrating on:

- types and processes of modelling used by students to solve a problem;
- clarity of understanding of organisation using the concepts of cells and particles;
- developing the students' perception of the relationship between micro-processes and macro-function of a system such as an organ or material;
- developing the concept of energy transfer causing change from a manipulative model to a mathematical model;
- promotion of the use of spreadsheets to model and predict events;
- developing the mathematical analysis of graphs using transferable skills.

CHAPTER 13

Enrichment by Use of Masterclasses/ Cross-curricular Projects

Structure for a masterclass

Teachers need to research carefully a real-life problem to which there are only partial solutions but the knowledge is within the range of the students by research. Reflection and discussion will enable them to develop a better appreciation of the way the knowledge can help to point them in the direction of a solution.

Next teachers need to identify books and websites to help the students in their research and make a list to 'drip-feed' them on the day of the masterclass if they begin to stall. It is better to ensure they can use both Internet and books. A good way of ensuring they cannot copy too much is to place credits on the paper and give them an amount they can use, say three sides maximum of A4 and any over that will cost 50 credits out of a total of 250 credits. At the end the group with the highest number of credits will be deemed an efficient group.

An outline of the structure of a masterclass is provided here. Use is made of high level thinking skills in relation to academic objectives focusing on concepts in a specific real-life context. Affective objectives are related to interpersonal and intrapersonal skills in individual group work and decision-making skills are related to evaluation. The timings relate to a full day's masterclass and are approximate.

Students are broken up into groups of four or five students each and the groups compete with each other to solve some problems.

Part one: Students – make yourself an expert (about 1.5 hours)

In this part we make use of research using ICT, the Internet and library searches, analysis thinking skills and individual intrapersonal skills linked to evaluation of information in relation to the focused objective.

Each pupil in a group is given a number and all students with that number from the collection of individual groups research a different part of the topic. They must make decisions on whether they will share the task with others from a different group with the same number. The sum of this research allows the groups to have enough information to solve the problems.

Part two: Students – sharing to solve a problem (45 minutes + 2.5 hours)

In this part we make use of communication, application, synthesis and evaluation thinking skills in relation to problem solving. The pupils come together in their individual groups and are given a set of problems to solve.

The first action for each group is a mapping exercise in which they link the information they have found to differing aspects of the work.

Second they brainstorm possible solutions and delegate differing people to selected aspects of the problem-solving activities.

Third they attack the problem, working against the clock to prepare a presentation, which can be a mixture of poster, model or ICT.

Part three: Students – evaluating the solutions (30 minutes)

In this last part they present their solution and evaluate each other's solution by awarding 1–5 points for each part with respect to:

- Communication – Does the presentation give me all the information I need?
- Use of information – Has the team made good use of all the information?
- Presentation – Is the final presentation attractive and effective?

An example of this style of masterclass is given below:

Masterclass – whole day science/technology/English: Notes for teachers

This challenge focuses upon osteoporosis as the topic and upon the skills of reading and interpreting information (links to the **National Curriculum English** are Reading 1a, b, c, g, j, 4a, b, c, d, 6 and **National Curriculum ICT** 1a, b, 2a, 3a, 3c, 4d, 5b) to solve a real-life problem.

Another area developed in the day's activity is that of cooperative learning and group working (links to the **National Curriculum English** are Speaking and Listening 2a, b, 3a, 3b, 3c, 3d, 3e, 5). This will require the students to be put into groups of five.

The information concentrates upon health issues and a disease that has its origins in either the genes of an individual, poor diet or inappropriate lifestyle and more surprisingly space flight (links to the **National Curriculum Science** are Sc2 1a, b, c, e, 2a, 2e, 2f, 4a; Sc4 3b, c, 4c, 4e).

The challenge presents the student with much information about osteoporosis and some information about astronauts' susceptibility to the disease because of microgravity (links to the **National Curriculum Science** are Sc1 1a, c, 2a, b, d, e, i, j, k, m, o, p). There is much information that will need some discussion and sorting. The answering of the questions should come first and then they should attempt the handouts by working in groups to design a device to help astronauts survive space flight without too much bone loss (links to the **National Curriculum Technology** are Te 1a, b, c, d, f, 3a, i, 6c). Finding out what words mean is an important activity in science and can help students to understand some of the ideas parcelled in the word (links to the **National Curriculum English** are Speaking and Listening 6f).

Thinking skills being used are:

Skill		
Knowledge –	**Remembering**	In familiar concrete experiential situations these constitute **Lower level thinking skills**
Comprehension –	**Understanding**	
Application –	**Applying**	
Analysis –	**Analysing**	In unfamiliar abstract situations these constitute **Higher level thinking skills**
Synthesis –	**Creating**	
Evaluation –	**Evaluating**	

Useful websites

Space flights and osteoporosis can be found on:

www.nasa.gov/women/health/aging.html

www.gsfc.nasa.gov

www.spacelink.nasa.gov

Osteoporosis can be found on:

http://courses.washington.edu/bonephys

www.osteoporosis.ca/

www.osteo.org

www.nof.org

www.merckmedicus.com/pp/us/hcp/diseasemodules/modules.jsp

Gravity, material research and space flight can be found on:

www.msfc.nasa.gov/NEWMSFC/slg.html

www.kapili.com/physics4kids/motion/index.html

http://physicsweb.org/resources/

www.ask.co.uk

www.exploratorium.edu/exploring/index.html

www.science.nasa.gov/newhome/headlines/msad15jul97_1.htm

More background notes on the topic for the teacher

After fertilisation a bundle of cells settle inside the thick wall of the uterus. This developing foetus is composed of cells from a common cell-type called a **blastomere**. This ball of developing cells, called a **blastocyst**, soon starts to form specialised cells, (*blasto* comes from the Greek meaning germ or sprout).

During the human gestation period bone cells form from osteoblast cells (*osteo* from the Greek word meaning bone) by forming special proteins (Greek *proteios* meaning primary), osteocalcin and osteopontein. These proteins give the bone cells characteristics such as hardness and rigidity. The fast production of bone cells continues through childhood and into young adulthood when it slows down. Bone production is most efficient when the person is involved in load-bearing exercise particularly against gravity (Latin *gravitas* meaning weight, *gravis* meaning heavy).

Production of poor bone cells can lead to a disease called osteoporosis. This condition means the bones become brittle and fragile due to the loss of bone tissue.

It can occur due to deficiency of vitamin D or calcium. It also occurs in older people due to changes in special chemicals called hormones (Greek *hormon* meaning to set in motion) that regulate the body.

Osteoporosis disease is more common in women than in men. Among women aged 65, 27% suffer from the disease while in men of the same age only 2.7% suffer the disease. Osteoporosis can be inherited but the possibilities of developing the disease can be slowed or reduced by good diet in teenage years. Some of the common signs of osteoporosis are loss of height with age and stooping from the shoulders.

In space the gravity is reduced to one-millionth of that on Earth and it is known as microgravity. When an astronaut goes into space the bone producing cells slow down and the astronaut's bones start to become deficient in bone chemicals.

Work carried out on special space flights like STS-81 to investigate this indicates astronauts lose 1–4% of their weight-bearing bone material for each month spent in space. Once the bone loss is greater than 20% then bones will fracture during ordinary load-bearing activities.

Recently there has been further research in France for the European Space Agency where volunteers have stayed in specially designed beds to simulate weightlessness for a number of months. In the USA they have designed a special piece of apparatus that will stimulate the muscles by electric impulse to make the muscles work against a stress and tension activity.

Student sheet – structure of masterclass day

Objectives

- Work on one's own and cooperatively in a team;
- Research, identify important information and apply new knowledge to solve a problem;
- Think creatively to produce a number of resources for others;
- Think critically to evaluate and select material for others and to solve a problem.

Session 1: Introduction to the research activity – 'Make yourself an expert' (about 1.5 hours)

Students to work in groups of five. Each student will take a numbered card out of an envelope that will identify the question they need to research. Each student will then use the Internet, library and dictionaries to research and make notes on one of the following:

1. Many of the words concerned with **osteoporosis** start with *osteo*. This is a 'fossil' word, one which has some idea of its meaning in the name but it is an old word coming from another language like the words **blastos**, **protein**, **gravity** and **hormone**. Find out what the words in bold mean and the language they come from. Others in your group will need to understand these words so build a glossary for your group of these and any other words you think will be necessary to the project.
2. Proteins are special chemicals produced by living things to help build the body materials. What proteins do osteoblast cells produce to give bones rigidity and hardness? When does production start in the human body? Identify the process of bone building and bone destruction.
3. Why does osteoporosis affect older people more than younger adults? What is the ratio of men to women who, at 65, suffer from osteoporosis? Are there any differences for different ethnic groups? Why is osteoporosis so important for people travelling into space for long periods of time?
4. Which groups of people should health advisers aim advice adverts at and why do you think that? Explain why the advice will be different for differing ages. Is there any difference by ethnicity?
5. A flight to Mars is estimated to take 30 months. What will be the dangers to the astronauts and how much bone would they expect to lose? Do materials such as elastic and magnets work in space as they do on Earth? Why is gravity such an important thing to consider in space and what are the effects of micro-gravity on human bones?

Session 2: 'Share the material with the group and collect some more from space' (45 minutes)

In this session the students will re-form in their groups and will have an introduction to the problem of living in space from the biology teacher. This will set the scene and establish some of the interconnections relating the problem to living in space. This will be followed by a group 'share and tell' session during which the group will need to identify the pieces of information that are important to the solution of the problem.

Session 3: Practical activity – 'Designing and solving problems' (2.5 hours)

In this session the students will work as a group and attempt to solve three practical problems by building small models using card, elastic bands and wood dowels and designing an exercise regime and two posters or handouts.

The students will need access to their notes to allow them to apply their research and science to their solutions. The models do not need to work but they must provide some design idea so they will need to be displayed with a scientific explanation of how they work.

The problems are:

1. Design a machine for exercising that would create weight-bearing or stress and tension exercise. Remember there is little gravity in space so weight training would not be a solution and neither would any machine relying on weights to create tension for muscles to work against and make the bones feel stress. Also

remember the human body undergoes changes that affect our efficiency to exercise. The change we are trying to reverse is the break-up of bone balanced against the build-up of bone. Also we have to take into account the physiological changes to the body during space flight. You will need to consider an exercise regime so all muscles are exercised.

2. Design three informative posters:
   - one for 9/10 year olds;
   - another for your parents to help them understand the disease and help them lessen their chances of contacting the condition;
   - one for students studying the science of space flight and osteoporosis.

   Remember osteoporosis can be genetic but it can also develop in people who do not have an appropriate diet. Such things as – poor exercise, poor diet, bad dieting to lose weight in teenage years, increased salt intake, increased alcohol intake, smoking, low protein diet, increased caffeine intake – can increase the likelihood of osteoporosis developing.

For the last 15 minutes of this session clear up and prepare the presentation of posters/models.

Evaluation of each group's posters (20 minutes)

Each set of posters will be displayed with a sheet of A4 paper attached to it. Each group will go round each other's poster and make constructive comments on each set of posters. They will award marks out of five for accuracy of science, presentation and use of language. They may not award any points to their own but must respond to each group with points and a simple comment to support the value given.

Concluding ideas and summary (10 minutes)

Students will identify the areas that presented them with the biggest challenge, the areas they found the most interesting and what they feel they have learnt from the day. Think back over the day and answer each of the following questions with a short sentence:

1. What activity presented the biggest challenge and made you think the most during the day?
2. What activity did you find the most interesting and would have liked to have spent more time on during the day?
3. What do you feel you have learnt from the day's activity?

Design brief for teachers

Design a masterclass around the following topic:

> A company has discovered a technique of mineral production that has as a by-product the element antimony. Antimony has had a long career in the history of man from the ancient Egyptians to the present day.

The following example of an evaluation form will supply some information about the metacognition development and response to the activity. Students also value a certificate citing the objectives achieved. An example of a suitable certificate is shown after the evaluation form.

Example of an evaluation form for use as part of masterclass

Evaluation

Student's name:

1. What activity presented the biggest challenge and made you think the most during the day?

2. What activity did you find the most interesting and would have liked to have spent more time on during the day?

3. What do you feel you have learnt more about from the day's activity?

4. Did you find working in a group an easy thing and why do you say that?

Example of a masterclass certificate

Certificate

This is to certify that

....

on

....

of

....School

successfully completed the following objectives:

- work on one's own and cooperatively in a team;
- research and apply new knowledge to solve a problem;
- think creatively to produce a number of resources for others;
- think critically to evaluate, select materials and solve a problem;

in a masterclass project on
space travel, NASA and osteoporosis.

Signed:

Tutor

References

Allen, L. S. and Gorski, R. A. (1991) 'Sexual dimorphism of the anterior commissure and massa inter media of the human brain', in *Journal of Comparative Neurology* **312**:97–104.

ASE Working Party (1994) *Models and Modelling in Science Education*. Hatfield: Association for Science Education.

Assessment Reform Group (1999) *Assessment for Learning: Beyond the black box*. Cambridge: University of Cambridge School of Education.

Bedfordshire Education Service (1988) *Bedfordshire Activities for Process Science*. Bedford: Bedfordshire TMRS.

Bellack, A., Kliebard, H., Hyman, R. and Smith, F. (1966) *The Language of the Classroom*. New York: Teachers College Press.

Bloom, B. S., Engelhart, M. D., Furst, E. J., Hill, W. H. and Kathwohl, D. R. (1956) *Taxonomy of Educational Objectives: The cognitive domain*. New York: Longmans Green.

Bulman, L. (1996) 'Pupils' perceptions of themselves as thinkers, learners and problem-solvers', *Educational and Child Psychology* **13**(3): 25–30.

Burden, R. L. (1998) 'Assessing children's perceptions of themselves as learners and problem-solvers', *School Psychology International* **19**, x–y.

Burke, J. (1996) *The Pinball Effect: How Renaissance water gardens made the carburettor possible*. Boston: Little, Brown.

Button, L. (1983) *Developmental Groupwork with Adolescents*. London: Hodder and Stoughton.

Buzan, T. (1993) *The Mind Map Book*. London: BBC Books.

Calvin, H. W. (1996) *How Brains Think: Evolving Intelligence, Then and Now* (Science Masters Series).

Carbo, M. and Hodges, H. (1988) 'Learning styles strategies can help students at risk', *Teaching Exceptional Children*, Summer, **20**(4): 55–58.

Catterell, R. B. (1987) *Intelligence: Its structure, growth and action*. Amsterdam: North Holland.

Centre for Management Creativity (2002) *LVT Thinking Skills Guidebook*. Settle: CMC.

Couper, H. and Henbest, N. (1996) *Black Holes*. London: Dorling Kindersley.

de Bono, E. (1989) *Teach Your Child to Think*. London: Penguin.

DES (1985) *Science 5–16: A statement of policy*. London: HMSO.

Driver, R., Squires, A., Rushworth, P. and Wood-Robinson, V. (1994) *Making Sense of Secondary Science*. London: Routledge.

Elliot, L. (1997) *Early Intelligence.* London: Penguin.

Ewy, C. A. (2003) *Teaching with Visual Frameworks.* London: Sage.

Fairbrother, R. (2000) 'Strategies for learning', in Monk, M. and Osborne, J. (eds) *Good Practice in Science Education.* Buckingham: Open University, 7–24.

Feuerstein, R. R. and Hoffman, M. (1980) *Instrumental Enrichment: An intervention programme for cognitive modifiability.* Illinois: Scot, Foreman.

Fisher, L. (2002) *How to Dunk a Doughnut: The science of everyday life.* London: Weidenfeld and Nicolson.

Flower, L. and Hayes, J. R. (1980) 'The dynamics of composing: making plans and juggling constraints', in Gregg, L. W. and Steinberg, E. R. (eds) *Cognitive Processes in Writing.* Hillsdale: Erlbaum, 33.

Fullick, P. and Ratcliffe, M. (eds) (1996) *Teaching Ethical Aspects of Science.* Ft. Lauderdale, FL: The Bassett Press.

Gardner, H. (1983) *Frames of Mind.* New York: Basic Books.

Gentner, D. and Stevens, A. L. (1983) *Mental Models.* Hillsdale: Erlbaum.

Gilden, D. L. and Proffitt, D. R. (1989) 'Understanding collision dynamics', *Journal of Experimental Psychology: Human Perception. Performance.* **15**, 372–83.

Goleman, D. (1995) *Emotional Intelligence.* London: Bloomsbury.

Gopnick, A. and Meltzoff, A. N. (1997) *Words, Thoughts and Theories.* Cambridge MA: MIT Press.

Green, S. (1994) *Principles of Biopsychology.* New York: Psychology Press.

Greenfield, S. (2000) *The Private Life of the Brain.* London: The Penguin Press.

Gregorc, A. F. (1979) 'Learning/teaching styles: their nature and effects', in *Student learning styles: Diagnosing and prescribing programs.* Reston, VA, National Association of Secondary School Principle.

Gregorc, A. F. (1984) 'Style as a symptom: A phenomenological perspective', *Theory into Practice*, **23**, 51–55.

Gresh, L. and Weinberg, R. (2002) *The Science of Superheroes.* New Jersey: John Wiley.

Gribbin, J. and Gribbin, M. (1997) *Richard Feynman: A life in science.* London: Viking.

Gunstone, R. and White, R. (1992) *Probing Understanding.* London: Falmer Press.

Halliday, M. A. K. and Hasan, R. (1980) *Language, Context, and Text: Aspects of language in a social-semiotic perspective.* Oxford: Oxford University Press.

Hoey, H. (1991) *Understanding Biology through Problem Solving.* London: Blackie.

Horsfall, P. and O'Brien, P. (2000) *Science Web Textbook 1.* Cheltenham: Nelson Thornes.

Horsfall, P., O'Brien, P., Macdonald, A. and Murphy, J. (eds) (2001–2003) *Science Web Textbooks 1, 2* and *3.* Cheltenham: Nelson Thornes.

Hughes, M. (1997) *Lessons are for Learning.* Stafford: Network Educational Press.

IEA (TIMSS) (1996/97) Science Achievement Reports for the Third International Mathematics and Science Study. Boston Hill: Centre for the Study of Testing, Evaluation and Educational Policy.

Inagaki, K. and Hatano, G. (1987) 'Young children's spontaneous personification as analogy', *Child Development* **58**, 1013–20.

Jensen, E. (1995/2000) *Brain Based Learning.* San Diego: The Brain Store.

Kempa, R. (1986) *Assessment in Science.* Cambridge: Cambridge University Press.

Keogh, B. and Naylor, S. (1999) *Using Concept Cartoons in Science.* Hatfield: Association for Science Education.

Kolb, D. A. (1984) *Experiential Learning.* Englewood Cliffs, NJ: Prentice-Hall.

Lassaline, M. E. and Murphy, G. L. (1998) 'Alignment and category learning', *Journal of Experimental Psychology: Learn. Memory. Cognition.* **24**, 144–60.

Learners' Cooperative (1996) *The Learners' Cooperative Differentiation Manual.* Plymouth: Learners' Cooperative.

Lewin, R. (1987) *A Practical Problem Solvers Handbook for Teachers and Students.* Reading, Berkshire: Royal County of Berkshire.

Mayer, J. D. and Salovey, P. (1997) 'The intelligence of emotional intelligence', *Intelligence* **17**, 433–42.

McCarthy, B. (1982) *The 4MAT System.* Arlington: Excel Publishing.

McGuinness, C. (1999) *From Thinking Skills to Thinking Classrooms: A review and evaluation of approaches for developing students' thinking.* Nottingham: DfEE Publications.

McGuinness, C., Curry, C., Greer, B. *et al.* (1996) *Final Report on the ACTS Project: Phase 1*: Belfast: Northern Ireland CCEA.

Millar, R. (ed.) (1989) *Doing Science: Images of science in science education.* Brighton: Falmer Press.

Miller, G. A. (1956) 'The magical number seven plus or minus two. Some limits on our capacity for processing information', *Psychological Review* **63**, 81–97.

Novak, J. D. and Gowin, D. R. (1984) *Learning How to Learn.* Cambridge: Cambridge University Press.

O'Brien, P. (1997) *Gifted Students in Science Project: Part of the Berkshire Improvement in Standards Initiative: A report on issues for action.* Berkshire: Berkshire Education Quality Assurance.

O'Brien, P. (2000) 'The Body's Chemical Factory', in Solomon, J. (ed.) *Science Web Reader – Biology,* 12–15. Cheltenham: Nelson Thornes.

O'Brien, P. (2002) 'Analysis of cognitive ability test data to inform teaching and learning', a research paper for Department for Education and Skills IQEA Project. London: DfES.

O'Brien, P. (2003) *Use of Cognitive Ability Test Data to Inform Teaching.* London: nferNelson Granada Learning.

Open University (1999) *Galapagos: Adaptation and evolution on islands* and *A Geological Field Trip* (two titles on a single CD-Rom). Milton Keynes: Open University.

Perkins, D. N. (1995) *Outsmarting IQ: The emerging science of learnable intelligence.* New York. Free Press.

Pogrow, S. (1994) 'Helping students who "just don't understand",' *Educational Leadership,* Journal of Department of Supervision and Curriculum Development, NEA **52**(30): 62.

QCA (1999) *National Curriculum Scheme of Work for Science Key Stage 3: Unit 7a Cells.* London: The Stationery Office.

Renzulli, J. S. (1978) 'What makes giftedness? Re-examining a definition', *Phi Delta Kappa* **60** 180–4.

Resnick, L. B. (1987) *Report of the Working Party on Thinking Skills.* Washington: US National Research Council.

Richardson, K. (1999) *The Making of Intelligence.* London: Weidenfeld and Nicholson.

Roberts, R. M. (1989) *Serendipity: Accidental discoveries in science.* New York: John Wiley.

Rose, C. (1985) *Accelerated Learning.* Aylesbury: Accelerated Learning Systems.

Shayer, M. and Adey, P. (1981) *Towards a Science of Science Teaching.* London: Heinemann.

Shayer, M. and Adey, P. (1994) *Thinking Science INSET.* London: Kings College/BP.

Sizmur, S. and Ashby, J. (1997) *Introducing Scientific Concepts to Children.* Slough: NFER.

Smith, P., Fernandes, C. and Strand, S. (2001) *Technical Manual: Cognitive Abilities Test 3.* Windsor: nferNelson.

Solomon, J. (ed.) (2000) *Science Web Readers – Biology, Chemistry and Physics.* Cheltenham: Nelson Thornes.

Stannard, R. J. (1994) *Uncle Albert and the Quantum Quest.* London: Faber and Faber.

Sternberg, R. J. (1985). *Beyond IQ – A Triarchic Theory of Human Intelligence.* Cambridge: Cambridge University Press.

Sternberg, R. J. (1990) *Metaphors of the Mind.* Cambridge: Cambridge University Press.

Sternberg, R. J. (1994) 'Allowing for thinking styles', *Educational Leadership,* **52**(3), 36–40.

Sutton, C. (1992) *Words, Science and Learning.* Buckingham: Open University.

Sutton, C. (1996) 'The scientific model as a form of speech', in Welford, G., Osborne, J. and Scott, P. (eds) *Research in Science Education in Europe.* London: Falmer Press, 143–52.

Vernon, P. E. (1961) *The Structure of Human Abilities,* 2nd edition. London: Methuen.

Vygotsky, L. S. (1962) *Thought and Language.* New York: Wiley.

Vygotsky, L. S. (1978) *Mind in Society.* Cambridge, MA: Harvard University Press.

Wellington, J. and Osborne, J. (2001) *Language and Literacy in Science Education.* Buckingham: Open University.

Winner, E. (1996). *Gifted Pupils: Myths and Realities.* New York. Basic Books.

Wittgenstein, L. (1967) *Philosophical Investigations* (Translated by G. E. M. Anscombe). Oxford: Blackwell.

Woolnough, B. (1994) *Effective Science Teaching.* Buckingham: Open University.

Wray, D. and Lewis, D. E. (1997) *Extending Literacy: Children reading and writing non-fiction.* London: Routledge.

Index